Directory

EMPLOYERS' ASS

TRADE UNIONS,

JOINT ORGANISATIONS, &c.

£1.80

LONDON: HMSO

*4
*production should be made to HMSO
1994

ISBN 0 11 361334 2

HMSO

Standing order service

Placing a standing order with HMSO BOOKS enables a customer to receive future editions of this title automatically as published.

This saves the time, trouble and expense of placing individual orders and avoids the problem of knowing when to do so.

For details please write to HMSO BOOKS (PC 11C), Publications Centre, PO Box 276, London SW8 5DT and quoting reference 17.02.012.

The standing order service also enables customers to receive automatically as published all material of their choice which additionally saves extensive catalogue research. The scope and selectivity of the service has been extended by new techniques, and there are more than 3,500 classifications to choose from. A special leaflet describing the service in detail may be obtained on request.

The price of this report has been set to make some contribution to the preparation costs incurred at the Employment Department

Introduction

This Directory is designed to provide comprehensive lists of United Kingdom organisations whose objects include the negotiation of, or making of recommendations on, wages and working conditions, or which provide representatives on organisations which are so concerned. Associations whose interest in these matters is limited to affiliation to negotiating bodies, and those with purely commercial, technical, educational, social or political objects are excluded. The entries show the names of the organisations, and the names, addresses, and telephone numbers of the secretaries or similar officials.

The organisations are grouped according to the industries in which they function, the order being that of the Standard Industrial Classification, 1980 revision.

In general, within each industry group, national organisations are given last. Where there are separate organisations in Scotland or Northern Ireland, these are arranged in that order, after entries for Great Britain. So far as is practicable, affiliated associations are indented below the association to which they are affiliated. Subject to the foregoing, the arrangement within each group is alphabetical.

The Directory has been reprinted in accordance with the latest information available at the time of going to press. The Department is always glad to receive particulars of alterations, which should be forwarded to the address below. The Directory is issued, in full, twice a year.

DEPARTMENT OF EMPLOYMENT,
Statistics Division B2,
Room 212
East Lane
RUNCORN
Cheshire
WA7 2DN

Employers' Associations

Contents

Page

Employers' Associations

So far as possible, the following list is confined to Associations whose objects, include the negotiation of wages and working conditions, the intention being to exclude, as a rule, Chambers of Commerce, of Agriculture and of Shipping, Trade Protection and Insurance Societies, and all Associations with purely commercial or technical objects. It has, however, not always been easy to make the distinction, and the Department would welcome any information with regard to organisations wrongly included or omitted.

AGRICULTURE, FORESTRY, FISHING

Agriculture

National Farmers' Union
The Secretary, 22 Long Acre, London, WC2E 9LY. Tel. 071-235 5077

National Farmers' Union of Scotland. Area Executive Committees
The Secretary, 17 Grosvenor Crescent. Edinburgh, EH12 5EN. Tel. 031-337 4333

Ulster Farmers' Union
The Secretary, 475–477 Antrim Road, Belfast, BT15 3DA. Tel. 370222 (STD code 0232)

Fishing

Aberdeen Fishing Vessel Owners' Association Limited
The Secretary, 5 Albert Quay, Aberdeen, AB1 2QA Tel. 29283 (STD code 0224)

Fleetwood Fishing Vessel Owners' Association Limited
The Secretary, 190–192 Dock Street, Fleetwood, Lancashire, FY7 6NU. Tel. 3532 (STD code 039-17)

Grimsby Fishing Vessel Owners' Association
The Secretary, Rinovia Buildings, Farringdon Road, Fish Docks, Grimsby, South Humberside, DN31 3TE. Tel. 355441 (STD code 0472)

Hull Fishing Industry Association
The Secretary c/o J Marr Limited, Marr Building, St. Andrew's Dock, Hull, HU3 4PN. Tel. 27873 (STD code 0482)

Lowestoft Fishing Vessel Owners' Association Limited
The Secretary, Star Buildings, Beach Road, Lowestoft, Suffolk, NR32 1D2 Tel. 0502 4312

Trawler Owners' Association Limited
The Secretary, The Docks, Milford Haven, Pembrokeshire. Tel. 2125

ENERGY SUPPLY

Coal

North East Association of Small Mines
The Secretary, 2nd Floor, 3 The Bigg Market, Newcastle upon Tyne, NE1 1UN. Tel. 091 221 0274

EXTRACTION OF MINERALS AND ORES OTHER THAN FUELS

Stone, clay, sand and gravel

British Ball Clay Producers' Federation Limited
The Secretary, Park House, Courtenay Park, Newton Abbot, Devon, TQ12 4PS. Tel. 332345 (STD code 0626)

Central Scotland Whinstone Association
H. G. Davidson and Company, 27 Crathie Drive, Glenmavis, Airdrie ML6 0NR. Tel. Airdrie 51363

Stone, clay, sand and gravel *(continued)*

China Clay Association
The Secretary, John Keay House, St. Austell, Cornwall, PL25 4DJ. Tel. *74482 (STD code 0726)*

County Derry and North Antrim Quarry Owners' Association
The Secretary, Whitehall Chambers, 43 New Row, Coleraine, County Londonderry. Tel. *2164 (STD code 0265)*

East Scotland Quarrymasters' Association
H. G. Davidson and Company, 27 Crathie Drive, Glenmavis, Airdrie ML6 0NR. Tel. *Airdrie 51363*

Kentish Ragstone Association
c/o Levick and Company, Accountants, West Hill, 61 London Road, Maidstone, Kent, ME16 8TX. Tel. *0622 59121*

Natural Slate Quarries Association
The Secretary, 26 Store Street, London, WC1E 7BT. Tel. *071 323 3770*

North Midlands Lime and Limestone Association
The Secretary, 2 Paradise Street, Sheffield, S1 1UE. Tel. *724341 (STD code 0742)*

Northern Ireland Quarry Owners' Association
The Secretary, c/o Jackson Andrews and Co., 48 High Street, Belfast, BT1 2BY. Tel. *233152 (STD code 0232)*

Sand and Gravel Association Limited
The Secretary, 1 Bramber Court, 2 Bramber Road, London, W14 9PB. Tel. *071-381 8778*

Silica and Moulding Sands Association
The Secretary, 19 Warwick Street, Rugby, Warwickshire, CV22 3DH. Tel. *Rugby (0788) 73041*

South-Western Roadstone Employers' Federation
The Secretary, Warren House, Bath Road, Upper Langford, Bristol BS18 7EB. Tel. *(0934) 852269*

METAL MANUFACTURE

National Metal Trades Federation
The Secretary, Savoy Tower, 77 Renfrew Street, Glasgow, G2 3BZ. Tel. *041-332 0826*

Welsh Engineers' and Founders' Association
The Secretary, 11 St. James' Gardens, Swansea, SA1 6DY. Tel. *472837 (STD code 0792)*

MANUFACTURE OF NON-METALLIC MINERAL PRODUCTS

Bricks, Fireclay and Refractory Goods

Calcium Silicate Brick Association
11 White Lion House, Town Centre, Hatfield, Hertfordshire. Tel. *Hatfield 71580*

National Federation of Clay Industries Limited
The Secretary, R. E. Jarrett, Federation House, Station Road, Stoke on Trent ST4 2SA. Tel. *(0782) 744631*

Clay Pipe Development Association Limited
The Secretary, Drayton House, 30 Gordon Street, London, WC1H 0AU. Tel. *071-388 0025*

East Midlands Brick Association
The Secretary, c/o Baker Tilly, Scottish Life House, 154 Great Charles Street, Birmingham, B3 3HN. Tel. *021 233 2323.*

Northern Brick Federation
The Secretary, New Oxford House, 16 Waterloo Street, Birmingham B2 5UG. Tel. *021-643 3451*

Bricks, Fireclay and Refractory Goods *(continued)*

Scottish Employers' Council for the Clay Industries
The President, Gisgol Bricks Ltd, Bergius House, 20 Clifton Street, Glasgow, G3 7XA. Tel. *041 332 3342.*

Southern Brick Federation
The Secretary, c/o The Brick Development Association, 19 Grafton Street, London, W1

Stourbridge Firebrick Association
The Secretary, 11 St. James's Road, Dudley, West Midlands, DY1 1HP. Tel. *53285 (STD code 0384)*

North of Ireland Brickmakers' Association
Atkinson and Boyd, Chartered Accountants, 11 Donegall Square South, Belfast, BT1 5JF. Tel. *222861 (STD code 0232)*

Refractory Contractors Association
135 Rotherhithe Street, London SE16 4NF. Tel. *071 231 7122*

Refractory Users Federation
The Secretary, Suites 101-105 (5th Floor) Kent House, 87 Regent Street, London W1R 7HF; Tel. *071 734 5246*

Glass and Ceramic Goods

British Ceramic Manufacturers' Federation
The Secretary, Federation House, Station Road, Stoke-on-Trent, ST4 2SA. Tel. *744631 (STD code 0782)*

British Electro-Ceramic Manufacturers' Association
The Secretary, Federation House, Station Road, Stoke-on-Trent, ST4 2SA. Tel. *744631 (STD code 0782)*

Glass and Glazing Federation
The Secretary, 40–48 Borough High Street, London, SE1 1XB. Tel. *071-403 7177*

Scottish Glass Association
The Secretary, 13 Woodside Crescent, Glasgow, G3 7UP. Tel. *041-332 7144*

Stourbridge Crystal Glass Manufacturers' Association
The Secretary, P.O. Box 15 Blythe House, 134 High Street, Brierley Hill, West Midlands, DY5 3BG. Tel. *76411/5 (STD code 0384)*

Yorkshire Glass Manufacturers' Association
The Secretary, Sovereign House, South Parade, Leeds, LS1 1HQ. Tel. *(0532) 83200*

Miscellaneous Building Materials

British Precast Concrete Federation
The Secretary, 60 Charles Street, Leicester, LE1 1FB. Tel. *536161 (STD code 0533)*

Scottish Pre-Cast Concrete Manufacturers' Association
Graham Marr and McLachlan, Solicitors, 9 Princes Street, Falkirk, FK1 1LS. Tel. *22088 (STD code 0324)*

British Ready Mixed Concrete Association
The Secretary, 1 Bramber Court, 2 Bramber Road, London W14 9PB. Tel. *071-381 6582*

Master Carvers' Association
The Secretary, 26/34 Danbury Street, Islington, London N1. Tel. *081 502 4529*

Mastic Asphalt Council and Employers' Federation
See under Civil Engineering Contracting (page 24)

Slag Employers' Association
The Secretary, John Hadfield House, Dale Road, Matlock, Derbyshire. Tel. *0629-3456*

CHEMICAL INDUSTRY

Chemical Industries Association Limited
The Secretary, Kings Buildings, Smith Square, London SW1P 3JJ. Tel. *071-834 3399*

Chemical Industry *(continued)*

Paintmakers Association of Great Britain Limited
> *The Secretary, Alembic House, 93 Albert Embankment, London, SE1 7TY.* Tel. *071-582 1185*

  Paint and Oil Section of the Glasgow Chamber of Commerce
> *The Secretary, 30 George Square, Glasgow, G2 1EQ.* Tel. *041-204 2121*

Society of British Printing Ink Manufacturers Limited
> *The Secretary, Pira House, Randalls Road, Leatherhead, Surrey KT22 7RU.* Tel. *0372 378628*

METAL GOODS, ENGINEERING AND VEHICLES

Vehicles, Aircraft and Aerospace

United Kingdom Joint Wages Board of Employers for the Vehicle Building Industry
> *The Secretary, 3 Shakespeare Road, Finchley, London, N13 1XE.* Tel. *081-349 2066*

Vehicle Builders' and Repairers' Association
> *The Secretary, Belmont House, 102 Finkle Lane, Gildersome Leeds, LS27 7TW,* Tel. *Leeds 538333 (STD code 0532)*

Shipbuilding and Repairing

Anglian Marine Industries Association
> *The Secretary, Harbour Road, Oulton Broad, Lowestoft, Suffolk, NR32 3LZ.* Tel. *0502 569663*

Belfast Shipbuilders' Association
> *The Secretary, c/o Harland and Wolff Limited, Queen's Road, Belfast, BT3 9DU.* Tel. *58456 Extension 307 (STD code 0232)*

British Shipbuilders
> *The Secretary, 12–18 Grosvenor Gardens, London, SW1W 0DW.* Tel. *071-730 9600*

Hampshire Yacht and Boat Building Association
> *The Secretary, Boating Industries House, Vale Road, Oatlands, Weybridge, Surrey, KJ13 9NS.* Tel. *0932-54511*

Hull Marine & Industrial Contractors Association
> *Joint Secretaries, Samman House, Bowlalley Lane, Hull, North Humberside, HU1 1XT.* Tel. *0482 24976*

Kent Ship and Boat Building Employers' Association
> *The Secretary, c/o Smye Rumsby Ltd, 123 Snargate Street, Dover, Kent.* Tel. *Dover 201 187*

London Association of Shore Gang Contractors
> *The Secretary, c/o Scaflon Marine Ltd., (T/AS Grayspur) Tilbury Dock, Essex, RM18 7HB.*

London and District Scaling Employers' Association
> *The Secretary, Blackwall Engineering Works, Blackwall Way, London, E14 9QD.* Tel. *071-987 1625*

Medway Shiprepairers' Association
> *The Secretary, Boating Industry House, Vale Road, Outlands, Weybridge, Surrey, KT13 9NS*

Midland Boat Builders' Association
> *The Secretary, c/o A. M. Dickie and Sons Ltd., Garth Road, Bangor, Gwynedd.* Tel. *Bangor 53174/51784*

North-East and East Coast Master Riggers' and Ship Transporters' Association
> *The Secretary, 19 John Street, Sunderland, SR1 1JQ.* Tel. *74857 (STD code 0783)*

Scottish Boat Builders Association
> *The Secretary, Merchants House Buildings, 7 West George Street, Glasgow, G2 1BD.* Tel. *041-248 6161*

Shipbuilding and Repairing *(continued)*

Scottish East Coast Association of Shiprepairers and Shipbuilders
The Secretary, 74 South Street, St. Andrews, Fife, KY16 9JT. Tel. *0334-7 2104*

Shiprepairers and Shipbuilders Independent Association
The Secretary, 33 Catherine Place, London, SW1E 6DD. Tel. *071-828-0933*

Miscellaneous Engineering Production

Association of Drum Manufacturers
The Secretary, 115 High Street, Godalming, Surrey, GU7 1AQ. Tel. *22216 (STD code 048 68)*

British Button Manufacturers' Association
See under Other Manufacturing Industries (page 21)

British Lock Manufacturers' Association
The Secretary, Heath Street, Tamworth, Staffs, B79 7JH. Tel. *0827 52337*

British Surgical Trades Association (Incorporated)
The Secretary, 1 Webbs Court, Buckhurst Avenue, Sevenoaks, Kent, TN13 1LZ. Tel. *0732 458868*

Employers' Federation of Card Clothing Manufacturers
The Secretary, 39 Well Street, Bradford, West Yorkshire, BD1 5NL. Tel. *33286 (STD code 0274)*

Engineering Employers' Federation
The Secretary, Broadway House, Tothill Street, London, SW1H 9NQ. Tel. *071-222-7777*

   Central Lancashire Engineering Employers' Association
   The Secretary, Wynster House, 58 Chorley New Road, Bolton BL1 4AP. Tel. *34315* (STD 0204)

   Engineering Employers' East Midlands Association
   The Secretary, Regional Offices, Barleythorpe, Oakham, Rutland, Leicestershire, LE15 7ED. Tel. *Oakham 723711 (STD code 0572)*

   Engineering and Shipbuilding Employers' Association Yorkshire and Humberside
   The Secretary, Fieldhead, Sandhills, Thorner, Leeds, LS14 3DN. Tel. *Leeds 892671 (STD code 0532)*

   Engineering Employers' Association of South Lancashire, Cheshire and North Wales
   The Secretary, Charles House, Albert Street, Eccles, Manchester, M30 0PD. Tel. *061-788 9611*

   Engineering Employers' East Anglian Association
   The Secretary, 32 High Street, Hadleigh, Ipswich, IP7 5AP. Tel. *0473 827894*

   Engineering Employers' London Association
   The Secretary, Eela House, Station Road, Hook, Basingstoke, Hampshire, RG27 9TL. Tel. *0256 763969*

   Engineering Employers' Sheffield Association (*South Yorkshire and North Midlands*)
   The Secretary, Broomgrove, 59 Clarkehouse Road, Sheffield, S10 2LE. Tel. *0742-680671*

   Engineering Employers' Western Association
   The Secretary, Engineers' House, The Promenade, Clifton Down, Bristol, BS8 3NB. Tel. *Bristol 731471 (STD code 0272)*

   EEF West Midlands Association
   The Secretary, St James House, Frederick Road, Edgbaston, Birmingham, B15 1JJ. Tel. *021 456 2222*

   Mid-Anglian Engineering Employers' Association
   The Secretary, 16a Market Square, Sandy, Bedforshire, SG19 1LY. Tel. *681722 (STD code 0767)*

   National Engineering Construction Employers Association
   The Secretary, Broadway House, Tothill Street, London, SW1H 9NQ. Tel. *071–222 7777*

   North of England Engineering Employers' Association
   The Secretary, Derwent House, Town Centre, District 1, Washington, Tyne and Wear, NE38 7SR. Tel. *091 416 5656*

Miscellaneous Engineering Production (*continued*)

North West Lancashire Engineering Employers' Association
The Secretary, 17 Moor Park Avenue, Preston Lancs. PR1 6AS. Tel. Preston 53518 (STD code 0772)

Scottish Engineering Employers' Association
The Secretary, 105 West George Street, Glasgow, G2 1QL. Tel. 041-221 3181

Engineering Employers' Federation Northern Ireland Association
The Secretary, 2 Greenwood Avenue, Belfast, BT4 3JJ. Tel. 0232-672490

Federation of Drum and Keg Merchants and Reconditioners
The Secretary, Dickens House, 15 Took's Court, London, EC4A 1LA. Tel. 071-831 7581

Metal Packaging Manufacturers Association
The Secretary, Elm House, 19 Elmshott Lane, Cippenham, Slough, Berkshire, SL1 5QS. Tel. 0628 605203

National Association of Farriers, Blacksmiths and Agricultural Engineers
The Secretary, Avenue R, 7th Street, N.A.C. Stoneleigh, Warwickshire, CV8 2LG. Tel. 0203 696595

North-East Coast Welding Employers' Association
The Secretary, Addison Street, North Shields, Tyne and Wear, NE29 6LS. Tel. 73198 (STD code 089 45)

Scottish Association of Master Blacksmiths
The Secretary, 3 Randolph Crescent, Edinburgh, EH3 7UD. Tel. 031-225 5851

Scottish Master Patternmakers' Association
Davidson and Workman, Chartered Accountants, 16 Royal Terrace, Glasgow, G3 7NZ. Tel. 041-332 8038

Scottish Sheet Metal Workers' (Employers') Association
The Secretary, 180 St. Vincent Street, Glasgow, G2 5SJ. Tel. 041-221 1211

Sheffield Lighter Trades Industrial Section
The Secretary, Light Trades House, 3 Melbourne Avenue, Sheffield, S10 2QJ. Tel. 663084 (STD code 0742)

British Cutlery and Silverware Association
The Secretary, Light Trades House, 3 Melbourne Avenue, Sheffield, S10 2QJ. Tel. 663084 (STD code 0742)

Sheffield Engineers' (Small) Tools Manufacturers' Association
The Secretary, Light Trades House, 3 Melbourne Avenue, Sheffield, S10 2QJ. Tel. 663084 (STD code 0742)

Sheffield Spoon and Fork Blank Manufacturers' Association
The Secretary, 179 Watt Lane, Sheffield, S10 5RD. Tel. 725792 (STD code 0742)

Wire and Wire Rope Employers' Association
The Secretary, 5 Cromwell Road, London, SW7 2HX Tel. 051 346 1566

FOOD, DRINK AND TOBACCO

Bacon and Meat Products

Bacon and Meat Manufacturers' Industrial Group
The Secretary, 18–19 Cornwall Terrace, London, NW1 4QP. Tel. 071-935-7980

Association of Scottish Bacon Curers
Spicer Watson and Company, 65 Renfield Street, Glasgow, G2 1NS. Tel. 041-331 1501

Glasgow and District Retail Fleshers Association
The Secretary, 67 Robske Road, Glasgow, G46 7ER. Tel. 041-638-1774

Midland Bacon Curers' Association
The Secretary, PO Box No. 6, Hall Street, Brierley Hill, West Midlands, DY5 3AH

Ulster Curers' Association
The Secretary, 2 Greenwood Avenue, Belfast, BT4 3JL. Tel. 656275 (STD code 0232)

Bacon and Meat Products *(continued)*

Belfast Casing Manufacturers' Association
> *The Secretary, c/o Stephenson Fat Refining Company (1968) Limited, P.O. Box 17, Havana Street, Belfast, BT14 7ET.* Tel. *745297 (STD code 0232)*

Milk Products

The Dairy Trade Federation Ltd
> *The Secretary, 19, Cornwall Terrace, London, NW1 4QP.* Tel. *071-486-7244*

Northern Ireland Proprietary Dairymen's Association
> *The Secretary, H. J. Johnston and Company, 133 Royal Avenue, Belfast, BT1 1FG.* Tel. *21995 (STD code 0232)*

Scottish Association of Milk Product Manufacturers
> *Thomson McLintock and Company, Chartered Accountants, 216 West George Street, Glasgow, G2 2PF.* Tel. *041-248 5181*

Brewing and Malting

Brewers Association of Scotland
> *The Secretary, 6 St. Colme St., Edinburgh EH3 6AD.* Tel. *031 225 4681*

Brewers' Society
> *The Secretary, CBE LLB, 42 Portman Square, London, W1H 0BB.* Tel. *071-486 4831*

Birmingham and Midland Counties Wholesale Brewers' Association
> *The Secretary, 2nd Floor, Link House, Halesowen, West Midlands, Birmingham, B63 3HT.*

East Anglian Brewers Association
> *The Secretary, 2 Lower Goat Lane, Norwich, NR2 1EL.*

East Midlands Brewers' Association
> *The Secretary, Arnold Chambers, 29 Forman Street, Nottingham, NG1 4AA.*

Northern Home Counties Brewers' Association
> *The Secretary, 42 Portman Square, London, W1H 0BB.* Tel. *071-486 4831*

North West and North Wales Brewers' Association
> *The Secretary, Bridgewater House, 23 Barton Road, Worsley, Manchester, M28 4PE.* Tel. *061-794 9714*

South Eastern Brewers' Association
> *The Secretary, 42 Portman Square, London, W1H 0BB.* Tel. *071-486 4831*

South Wales Brewers' Association
> *The Secretary, Brewers Offices, Cross Street, Caerphilly Road, Cardiff, CF4 4AS.*

West of England Brewers' Association
> *The Secretary, 16 Castle Street, Bridgwater, Somerset, TA6 3DB*

Yorkshire Brewers' Association
> *The Secretary, 56 Leeds Road, Tadcaster, North Yorkshire, LS24 9HB*

Malt Distillers' Association of Scotland
> *Grigor and Young, 1 North Street, Elgin, Morayshire, IV30 1UA.* Tel. *544077 (STD code 0343)*

Maltsters Association of Great Britain
> *The Secretary, Lindpet House, Market Place, Grantham, Lincs, NG31 6LD.* Tel. *Grantham 0476 72855*

Miscellaneous Food and Drink

British Herring Trade Association Limited
> *The Secretary, Advocate, 13 Bon-Accord Crescent, Aberdeen, AB9 1NQ.* Tel. *50347 (STD code 0224)*

British Soft Drinks Association Limited
> *The Secretary, 20/22 Stukeley Street, London, WC2B 5LR.* Tel. *071-430 0356*

Miscellaneous Food and Drink *(continued)*

Federation of Bakers
    The Director, 20 Bedford Square, London, WC1B 3HF. Tel. *071-580 4252*

  Federation of Bakers (Scottish Area)
    The Secretary, 100 Stamford Street, Glasgow. Tel. *041-554-7371*

  Northern Ireland Bakery Employers' Council
    The Secretary, Bainsdale, Ballymacash Road, Lisburn, BT28. Tel. *2183 (STD code 084 62)*

Food Manufacturers' Industrial Group
    The Secretary, 6 Catherine Street, London, WC2B 5JJ. Tel. *071-836-2460*

Incorporated National Association of British and Irish Millers Limited
    The Secretary, 21 Arlington Street, London, SW1A 1RN. Tel. *071-493 2521*

  East Midlands Association of Flour Millers
    The Secretary, c/o Whitworth Brothers Limited, Victoria Mills, Wellingborough, Northamptonshire, NN8 2DT. Tel. *76351 (STD code 0933 3)*

  North Eastern Group of Flour Millers
    Berridge Cappleman and Co., Chartered Accountants, Suffolk House, Silver Street, Hull, HU1 1JN. Tel. *225663*

National Association of Master Bakers, Confectioners and Caterers
    The Secretary, 21 Baldock Street, Ware, Herts, SG12 9DH. Tel. *0920 468061*

N.E. Association of Seed Crushing and Feed Mill Employers
    The Secretary, Samman House, Bowlalley Lane, Hull, HU1 1XT. Tel. *24976 (STD code 0482)*

Northern Ireland Grain Trade Association Limited
    The Secretary, c/o Muir and Addy, 7 Donegall Square West, Belfast, BT1 6LN. Tel. *26215 (STD code 0232)*

Scottish Association of Master Bakers
    The Secretary, Atholl House, 4 Torphichen Street, Edinburgh, EH3 8JQ. Tel. *031-229-1401*

Stornoway Master Bakers' Association
    The Secretary, 60 Bayhead Street, Stornaway, Isle of Lewis, Outer Hebrides, PA87 2DZ. Tel. *Stornoway 2733*

Tobacco

Tobacco Industry Employers' Association
    The Secretary, Glen House, Stag Place, London, SW1E 5AG. Tel. *071-828 2041*

TEXTILES

Woollen and Worsted

British Wool Federation
    60 Toller Lane, Bradford, West Yorkshire, BS8 9DA. Tel. *491241 (STD code 0274)*

Confederation of British Wool Textiles Ltd.
    The Secretary, Merrydale House, Roydsdale Way, Bradford, West Yorkshire, BD4 6SB. Tel. *0274 652207*

  Wool (and Allied) Textile Employers' Council
    60 Toller Lane, Bradford, West Yorkshire, BD8 9DA. Tel. *46739 (STD code 0274)*

Hebridean Spinners' Advisory Committee
    The Secretary, 20 Francis Street, Stornoway, Isle of Lewis, Outer Hebrides. Tel. *0851 4343*

Northern Ireland Wool Users' Association
    The Secretary, 13 Glendale Avenue North, Belfast, BT8 4LD

Woollen and Worsted (*continued*)

Scottish Woollen Industry
The Secretary, 45 Moray Place, Edinburgh, EH3 6EQ. Tel. *031-225 3149*

West of England Wool Textile Employers' Association
The Secretary, Lodgemore Mills, Stroud, Gloucestershire. Tel. *045 363373*

Worsted Spinners' Federation Limited
The Secretary, 60 Toller Lane, Bradford, West Yorkshire, BD8 9DA. Tel. *491241 (STD code 0274)*

Bradford and District Master Spinners' Association
The Secretary, 60 Toller Lane, Bradford, West Yorkshire, BD8 9DA. Tel. *491241 (STD code 0274)*

Halifax and Huddersfield Worsted Spinners' Federation
The Secretary, 60 Toller Lane, Bradford, West Yorkshire, BD8 9DA. Tel. *491241 (STD code 0274)*

Keighley and District Master Spinners' Association
The Secretary, 60 Toller Lane, Bradford, West Yorkshire, BD8 9DA. Tel. *491241 (STD code 0274)*

Wakefield and District Master Spinners' Association
The Secretary, 60 Toller Lane, Bradford, West Yorkshire, BD8 9DA. Tel. *491241 (STD code 0274)*

Hosiery and Other Knitted Goods

Hawick Knitwear Manufacturers' Association
(Director) 32 Commercial Road, Hawick, Roxburghshire, TD9 7EQ. Tel. *72983 (STD code 0450)*

Knitting Industries Federation Limited
The Secretary, 53 Oxford St, Leicester, LE1 5XY. Tel. *0533 541608*

Hinckley and District Knitting Industry Association
The Secretary, 37 Station Road, Hinckley, Leicestershire, LE10 1AP. Tel. *38771-2 (STD code 0455)*

Leicester and District Knitting Industry Association Limited
The Secretary, 53 Oxford Street, Leicester, LE1 5XY. Tel. *0533 541608*

Loughborough and District Hosiery Manufacturers' Association
The Secretary, 41 Granby Street, Loughborough, Leicester, LE11 3DU. Tel. *21 2890 (STD code 050 93)*

North Midlands Regional Council
The Secretary, 7 Gregory Boulevard, Nottingham, NG7 6NB. Tel. *621081*

Scottish Knitwear Association
The Secretary, 55 John Finnie Street, Kilmarnock, KA1 1HQ. Tel. *0563 23568*

Carpets

British Carpet Manufacturers' Association
The Secretary. 26 St. Jame's Square, London, SW1. Tel. *071-839-2145*

Kidderminster District Carpet Manufacturers' and Spinners' Association
The Secretary, c/o Brintons Ltd., P.O. Box 16, Exchange Street, Kidderminster, Worcestershire, DY10 1AG. Tel. *0562 820000*

Northern Area Carpet Manufacturers' Association
The Secretary, Firth Carpets Limited. P.O. Box 17, Clifton Mills, Brighouse, West Yorkshire, HD6 4EJ. Tel. *3371 (STD code 048 47)*

Scottish Carpet Manufacturers' Association
The Secretary, c/o Mitchells Johnston Hill and Hogan, 160 West George Street, Glasgow, G2 2JB. Tel. *041-331 1681*

Lace

British Lace Federation
(Director) Nottingham Chamber of Commerce and Industry, 395 Mansfield Road, Nottingham, NG5 2DL. Tel. *624624 (STD code 0602)*

Lace *(continued)*

British Leavers Lace Manufacturers' Association
> *The Secretary, c/o F. and C. Mason Ltd., Belper Street, Ilkeston, Derbyshire.* Tel. *(0602) 325031*

Scottish Lace and Window Furnishings Association
> *The Secretary, 1 Craigview Road, Newmilns, Ayrshire, KA16 9DQ.* Tel. *0560-20041*

Narrow Fabrics

British Federation of Narrow Elastic Manufacturers
> *The Secretary, British Federation of Narrow Elastic Manufacturers, 4th Floor, York House, 91 Granby Street, Leicester LE1 6EA.* Tel. *0533 551491*

British Federation of Trimmings and Braids Manufacturers
> *The Secretary, Bank House, 20 St. Edward Street, Leek, Staffordshire, ST13 5DS.* Tel. *386826 (STD code 0538)*

British Narrow Fabrics Association
> *The Secretary, 4–6 New Street, Leicester LE1 5NT.* Tel. *0533 545490*

Ribbon and Label Manufacturers Association
> *The Secretary, c/o Clothing and Footwear Institute, Albert Road, London, NW4 2JS.* Tel. *081-203-0191*

Tape and Webbing Manufacturers' Association
> *The Secretary, c/o Spicer and Pegler, P.O. Box 498, Derby House, 12–16 Booth Street, Manchester, M60 2ED.* Tel. *061-236 9721*

Cotton and Other Textiles

The Jute Importers Association Limited
> *The Secretary, c/o Taybank Works, 60 Arbroath Road, Dundee DD1 4EA.* Tel. *456504 (STD code 0382)*

Bridport Manufacturers' Association
> *The Secretary, The Court, Bridport, Dorset*

British Textile By-Products Association
> *The Secretary, Thorncliffe, 115 Windsor Road, Oldham, Lancs, OL8 1RQ.* Tel. *061 624 3611*

British Textile Employers' Association
> *The Secretary, Reedham House, 31 King Street West, Manchester, M3 2PF.* Tel. *061-834 7871*

Blackburn District Textile Manufacturers' Association
> *The Secretary, 4 St. Andrews Street, Blackburn, Lancs, BB1 8AE.* Tel. *0254 580248*

Bolton and District Textile Employers' Association
> *The Secretary, Lloyds Bank Chambers, Howell Croft North, Bolton, BL1 1QY.* Tel. *21511 (STD code 0204)*

Bury District Federation of Cotton Spinners and Manufacturers
> *The Secretary, 94 Manchester Road, Bury, Lancashire, BL9 0TH.* Tel. *061-764 1761*

Heywood and District Cotton Employers' Association Limited
> *The Secretary, c/o Lister-Mutual Yarns Ltd., Aspinall Street, Heywood, Lancs.* Tel. *0706-69061*

North East Lancashire Textile Manufacturers' Association
> *The Secretary, 4 St. Andrews Street, Blackburn, Lancs BB1 8AE.* Tel. *0254 580248*

Oldham and Rochdale Textile Employers' Association Limited
> *The Secretary, "Thorncliffe", 115 Windsor Road, Oldham, OL8 1RQ.* Tel. *061-624 3611*

Silsden and District Manufacturers' Association
> *The Secretary, Aire Valley Mills, Airedale Shed, Silsden, Keighley, W. Yorks.* Tel. *Steeton 52202*

Skipton and District Cotton and Rayon Manufacturers' Association
> *The Secretary, 23 Henry Street, Keighley, West Yorkshire, BD21 3DR.* Tel. *602341 (STD code 0535)*

Cotton and Other Textiles *(continued)*

Central Council of the Irish Linen Industry Limited
The Secretary, Lambeg Road, Lisburn, Northern Ireland, BT27 4RL. Tel. *Lisburn 77377*

Cordage and Net Manufacturers' (Employers) Association
The Secretary, c/o Rickard, Keen & Co., 9 Nelson Street, Southend on Sea. SS1 1EH.
Tel. *(0702) 347771*

Dyers' and Finishers' Association
60 Toller Lane, Bradford, West Yorkshire, Tel. *0274 491241*

The Flax and Linen Association (GB)
Robertson-Coupar and Co., 1 Bank Street, Dundee, DD1 1RN. Tel. *0382-25691*

Forfar and Kirriemuir Manufacturers' Association
The Secretary, c/o Don Brothers, Buist and Company Limited, St. James Road, Forfar,
Angus, DD8 2AL. Tel. *2171 (STD code 0307)*

Grimsby Net Manufacturers' Association
The Secretary, c/o Cosalt Limited, Fish Dock Road, Fish Docks, Grimsby, South
Humberside, DN31 3NW. Tel. *58931 (STD code 0472)*

Macclesfield Textile Manufacturers' Association
The Secretary, 11 Hall Close, Macclesfield, Cheshire, SK10 2HH. Tel. *0625 23554*

National Fillings Trades Association
The Secretary, 263A Monton Road, Monton, Eccles, Manchester, M30 9LF. Tel. *061 788*
9018

Nottingham Piece Goods Commission Dyers' and Finishers' Association
The Secretary, 7 College Street, Nottingham, NG1 5AS. Tel. *46377 (STD code 0602)*

Surgical Textiles Conference
The Secretary, c/o Vernon-Carus Ltd., Penwortham Mills, Factory Lane, Penwortham,
Preston Tel. *0772 744493*

United Kingdom Jute Goods Association Limited
The Secretary, 25 Balgores Lane, Romford. RM2 5JT. Tel. *0708 741967*

LEATHER AND LEATHER GOODS

British Leather Goods Manufacturers Association
The Secretary, 82 Borough High Street, London, SE1 1LL. Tel. *071-407 1582*

Industrial Leathers Federation
The Secretary, Leather Trade House, Kings Park Road, Moulton Park, Northampton,
NN3 1JD. Tel. *0604 494131*

Leather Producers' Association
The Secretary, Leather Trade House, Kings Park Road, Moulton Park, Northampton,
NN3 1JD. Tel. *Northampton (0604) 494131*

 East Midlands Leather Producers' Association
 The Secretary, Leather Trade House, 9 St. Thomas Street, London, SE1 9SA. Tel.
 071-407 1522

 London and District Leather Producers' Association
 The Secretary, Leather Trade House, 9 St. Thomas Street, London, SE1 9SA. Tel.
 071-407 1522

 Master Tanners' Association
 The Secretary, 80–86 Lord Street, Liverpool, L2 1TW. Tel. *051-708 9023*

 Northern Leather Producers' Association
 The Secretary, Leather Trade House, 9 St. Thomas Street, London, SE1 9SA. Tel.
 071-407 1522

 Western Leather Producers' Association
 The Secretary, Leather Trade House, 9 St. Thomas Street, London, SE1 9SA. Tel.
 071-407 1522

Leather and Leather Goods *(continued)*

Scottish Leather Producers' Association
c/o Anderson Fyfe Solicitors, 90 St. Vincent Street, Glasgow, G2 5UB. Tel. *041 248 4381*

Skinners' Association of Scotland
The Secretary, R. Legget and Sons Limited, Lochside Works, Kinghorn, Fife. Tel. *059-289 672*

United Kingdom Fellmongers' Association
The Secretary, 431 Wilmslow Road, Withington, Manchester, M20 9AD. Tel. *061-445 4235*

FOOTWEAR AND CLOTHING

Footwear

British Footwear Manufacturers Federation
The Secretary, 72 Dean Street, London, W1V 5HB. Tel. *071-437 5573*

Kingswood and District Boot Manufactuers' Association
The Secretary, c/o G. B. Britton Limited, Lodge Road, Kingswood, Bristol, BS15 1JB. Tel. *353637 (STD code 0272)*

Leeds and District Boot and Shoe Manufacturers' Association Limited
The Secretary, Gola Lamb Ltd., Bottom Boat Road, Stanley, Wakefield, W. Yorkshire, WF3 4AY. Tel. *823541 (STD code 0924)*

Leicester and County Footwear Manufacturers' Association *(a)*
The Secretary, c/o F. J. Palfreyman & Co Lmited, Linden Street, Leicester, LE5 5EB. Tel. *0533 733399*

London Footwear Manufacturers' Association
The Secretary, Unit 10D, Printing House Yard, 15A Hackney Road, London, E2 7PR. Tel. *071-739 1678*

Northamptonshire Footwear Manufacturers' Association
The Secretary, SATRA House, 249 Rockingham Road, Kettering, Northamptonshire, NN16 9JH. Tel. *0536 82175*

Norwich Footwear Manufacturers' Association
The Secretary, c/o Bally Shoe Factories (Norwich) Ltd, Hall Road, Norwich NR4 6DP. Tel. *761100 (STD code 0603)*

South Wales Footwear Manufacturers' Association
The Secretary, c/o Fiona Footwear, Queens Road, Industrial Estate, Bridgend, Mid Glamorgan, CF31 3YD. Tel. *0656 3438*

Scottish Footwear Manufacturers' Association
The Secretary, Footwear Supplies Limited, (Factories Division), Gleneagles Factory, Mill Street, Kilmarnock, KA1 4BG. Tel. *27373 (STD code 0563)*

Footwear Manufacturers' Association of Northern Ireland
The Secretary, c/o Down Shoes, Newry Road, Banbridge, Co. Down. Tel. *Banbridge 22271 Ext. 38*

Footwear Components Federation
A. C. Palmer and Company, Chartered Accountants, Provisional House, 37 New Walk, Leicester, LE1 6TU. Tel. *549818 (STD code 0533)*

Clothing, Hats and Gloves

Belfast Shirt and Collar Manufacturers' Association
The Secretary, 46 High Street, Lurgan, Craigavon, County Armagh, BT66 8AX. Tel. *Lurgan 2069 and 2270 (STD code 076 282)*

Bristol, West of England and South Wales Clothing Manufacturers' Association
The Secretary, 8/10 Whiteladies Rd., Clifton, Bristol BS8 1PD. Tel. *0272-30863*

British Clothing Industry Association Limited
The Secretary, 7 Swallow Place, London, W1R 7AA. Tel. *01-408 0020*

Clothing, Hats and Gloves *(continued)*

British Hat Guild
> *Joint Sec's., Chamber of Commerce Building, George Street West, Luton, LU1 2BT.* Tel. *23456 (STD code 0582)*
> *25 Brooks Mews, Davies Street, London W1Y 1LF.* Tel. *071-629 2964*

British Headwear Industries Federation
> *The Secretary, c/o Wilson & Stafford, Britannia Works, Cowlshill Road, Atherstone, Warwickshire, CV9 1BX.* Tel. *0827 717941*

Clothing Manufacturers Federation (1987)
> *The Secretary, Waterlinks House, Richard Street, Birmingham, B7 4AA,* Tel. *021 333 4080*

Cork Helmet Manufacturers' Association
> *The Secretary, c/o Hobson and Sons (London) Limited, 154–164 Tooley Street, London, SE1 2UA.* Tel. *071-407 2476*

Council of Making-up Trades in Northern Ireland
> *The Secretary, 46 High Street, Lurgan, Craigavon, County Armagh, BT66 8AX.* Tel. *Lurgan 2069 and 2270 (STD code 076 282)*

Federation of Merchant Tailors
> *The Secretary, Congress House, 55 New Cavendish Street, London W1M 7RE,* Tel. *071 486 0531*

Hebden Bridge and District Wholesale Clothiers' Association
> *The Secretary, Cresswell Crabtree and Sons, Chartered Accountants, Barclays Bank Chambers, Hebden Bridge, West Yorkshire, HX7 6AA.* Tel. *2431 (STD code 042 284)*

Huddersfield, Bradford and Districts Clothing Manufacturers' Association
> *The Secretary, Station Street Buildings, Huddersfield, HD1 1LN.* Tel. *21433 (STD code 0484)*

Irish Wholesale Clothing Manufacturers' Association
> *The Secretary, 46 High Street, Lurgan, Craigavon, County Armagh, BT66 8AX.* Tel. *Lurgan 2069 and 2270 (STD code 076 282)*

Lancashire and Cheshire Clothing Manufacturers' Association
> *The Secretary, 104 Tib Street, Manchester, M4 1LR.* Tel. *061-832 2195*

Leeds and Northern Clothing Manufacturers' Association
> *The Secretary, 4 South Parade, Leeds, LS1 5TZ.* Tel. *30595 (STD code 0532)*

Light Clothing Manufacturers' Association of Northern Ireland
> *The Secretary, 46 High Street, Lurgan, Craigavon, County Armagh, BT66 8AX.* Tel. *Lurgan 2069 and 2270 (STD code 076 282)*

London and District Clothing Manufacturers' Association
> *The Secretary, 14–16 Cockspur Street, London, SW1Y 5BL.* Tel. *071-930 9941*

Midland Clothing Manufacturers' Association
> *The Secretary, Wallis and Linnell Limited, Morley Street, Kettering, Northamptonshire, NN16 0DN.* Tel. *2445 (STD code 0536)*

National Association of Glove Manufacturers
> *Rutland House, 44 Masons Hill, Bromley, Kent BR2 9EQ.* Tel. *081-464-0131*

National Children's Wear Association of Great Britain and Northern Ireland
> *The Secretary, 40–42 Oxford Street, London, W1N 9FJ.* Tel. *071-636 1833*

Nottingham Chamber of Commerce and Industry Light Clothing Section
> *(Director) 395 Mansfield Road, Nottingham, NG5 2DL.* Tel. *45678 (STD code 0602)*

Scottish Clothing Manufacturers' Association
> *The Secretary, 2 Couston Holm Road, Glasgow, G43 1UE.* Tel. *041-632 9151*

Scottish Federation of Merchant Tailors
> *The Secretary, 3 Randolph Crescent, Edinburgh EH3 7UD.* Tel. *031 225 5851*

Scottish Light Clothing Manufacturers' Association
> *Connal and Bannatyne Ltd, 45 Finnieston St., Glasgow G3 8JX.* Tel. *041 221 1024*

Clothing, Hats and Gloves *(continued)*

Shirt Manufacturers' Federation (Northern Ireland)
>*The Secretary, 8 Shipquay Street, Londonderry.* Tel. *62858 and 63131. (STD code 0504)*

Yeovil and District Association of Glove Manufacturers
>*The Secretary, c/o Seager Bros. (Gloves) Ltd, Bristol Road, Sherborne, Dorset.* Tel. *0935 813666*

HOUSEHOLD AND MADE UP TEXTILES AND FURS

Artificial Flower Trade Association
>*P. J. Culpitt, G. T. Culpitt and Son Limited, 78–78 Town Centre, Hatfield, Hertfordshire.* Tel. *Hatfield 65516*

British Fur Trade Association (Incorporated)
>*The Secretary, 68 Upper Thames Street, London, EC4V 3AN.* Tel. *071-248 5947*

Handkerchief and Household Linens Association
>*The Secretary, c/o Spence Bryson, 41 Great Victoria Street, Belfast, BT2 7AD.* Tel. *0232 226464*

London Dressmakers and Allied Contractors Association
>*The Secretary, British Apparel Centre, 7 Swallow Place, London W1R 7AA.* Tel. *071-408 0020*

Tie Manufacturers' Association Limited
>*The Secretary, 14–16 Cockspur Street, London, SW1Y 5BL.* Tel. *071-930 0941*

Made-up Textiles Association Limited
>*The Secretary, Heath Street, Tamworth, Staffordshire, B79 7JH.* Tel. *0827 52337*

National Association of Sack Merchants and Reclaimers Limited
>*The Secretary, 76 Bellon Lane, Grantham, Lincolnshire.* Tel. *2201*

TIMBER AND FURNITURE

Association of British Plywood and Veneer Manufacturers
>*The Secretary, Riverside Industrial Estate, Morson Road, Ponders End, Enfield EN3 4TS.* Tel. *081-804-2424*

British Brush Manufacturers' Association
>*The Secretary, 35 Billing Road, Northampton, NN1 5DD.* Tel. *0604 22023*

British Exhibition Contractors Association
>*The Secretary, Kingsmere House, Graham Road, London, SW19 3SR.* Tel. *081-543 3888*

British Furniture Manufacturers' Federation
>*The Secretary, 30 Harcourt Street, London, W1H 2AA.* Tel. *071-724 0854*

High Wycombe Furniture Manufacturers' Society
>*The Secretary, Wycombe House, 9 Amersham Hill, High Wycombe, Buckinghamshire, HP13 6NR.* Tel. *23021 (STD code 0494)*

London and South Eastern Furniture Manufacturers' Association
>*The Secretary, 93 Great Eastern Street, London, EC2A 3JB.* Tel. *071-739 7916-7*

Midlands and North West Furniture Manufacturers' Association
>*The Secretary, 263A Monton Road, Monton, Eccles, Manchester, M30 9LF.* Tel. *061-788 9018*

National Bed Federation Limited
>*The Secretary, 251 Brompton Road, London, SW3 2EZ.* Tel. *071-589 4888*

Northern Furniture Manufacturers Association
>*The Secretary, Salisbury House, Salisbury Grove, Leeds, LS12 2AS.* Tel. *0532 794676*

Ulster Furniture Federation
>*The Secretary, 13 Carolsteen Avenue, Helen's Bay, Bangor, County Down.* Tel. *0247 852869*

Timber and Furniture *(continued)*

West of England and South Wales Furniture Manufacturers' Association
The Secretary, First Floor, York House, Bond Street, Bristol, BS1 3LQ. Tel. 420269 (STD code 0272)

British Timber Merchants Association (England and Wales)
The Secretary, Stocking Lane, Hughendon Valley, High Wycombe, Bucks, HP14 4JZ. Tel. 024-024 3602

Display Producers' and Screen Printers' Association Limited
The Secretary, 1st Floor, 243 Gray's Inn Road, London, WC1X 8RB. Tel. 071-837 2275

Fencing Contractors' Association
The Secretary, St. John's House, 23 St. John's Road, Watford, WD1 1PY. Tel. 0923 227236

National Association of Shopfitters
(Director) NAS House, 411 Limpsfield road, The Green, Warlingham, Surrey, CR3 9HA. Tel. Upper Warlingham 4961 (STD code 088 32)

North West Timber Trade Association
The Secretary, 263a Monton Road, Monton, Eccles, Manchester, M30 9LF. Tel. 061-788 9018

Scottish Furniture Manufacturers Association
The Secretary, Merchants House Buildings, 30 George Square, Glasgow, G2 1EG. Tel. 041-248 2375

Scottish National Federation of Packing Case Manufacturers
The Secretary, c/o A. M. Shaw, 7 Avon Place, Barnton, Edinburgh. Tel. 031-312 7015

Scottish Timber Trade Association
The Secretary, 24 Blythswood Square, Glasgow, G2 4QS. Tel. 041-226 5511

Sheffield Cabinet Case Manufacturers Association
The Secretary, 3 Melbourne Avenue, Sheffield, S10 2QJ.

Society of British Match Manufacturers
(Chairman) Bryant and May Ltd, Fairfield Road, Bow, London, E3 2QE. Tel. 081-980 4321

PAPER, PRINTING AND PUBLISHING

Pulp, Paper and Board

Association of Independent Wallcovering Manufacturers
The Secretary, c/o McGregor Wallcoverings, Eden Lane, Armstrong Road, Peterlee, Co. Durham SR8 5AF. Tel. 0783-862381

British Box and Packaging Association
P.O. Box No. 106, East Grinstead, West Sussex, RH19 2YL. Tel. 0342 313 534

British Fibreboard Packaging Association
The Director, 2 Saxon Court, Freeschool Street, Northampton NN1 1ST. Tel. 0604 21002

British Paper and Board Industry Federation Ltd.
The Secretary, 3 Plough Place, Fetter Lane, London EC4A 1Al. Tel. 071-353-5222

British Stationery and Office Products Federation
(Director) 6 Wimpole Street, London, W1M 8AS. Tel. 071-580 9526 and 3121

Envelope Makers and Manufacturing Stationers' Association
The Secretary, 6 Wimpole Street, London, W1M 8AS. Tel. 071-580 9256 and 3121

Multiwall Sack Manufacturers Employers' Association
The Secretary, Papermakers House, Rivenhall Road, Swindon, Wilts, SN5 7BD. Tel. 0793 886086

Wallcovering Manufacturers Association of Great Britain Limited
The Secretary, Alembic House, 93 Albert Embankment, London, SE1 7TY. Tel. 071-582 1185

Printing and Publishing

British Printing Industries Federation
The Secretary, 11 Bedford Row, London, WC1R 4DX. Tel. 071-242 6904

Graphic Reproduction Federation
The Secretary, 21 Whitefriars Street, London, EC4Y 8AL. Tel. 071-583 3122

Master Music Printers' and Engravers' Association
The Secretary, c/o Halstan and Company Limited, Plantation Road, Amersham,
Buckinghamshire, HP6 6HJ. Tel. 5525 (STD code 02403)

Newspaper Society
The Secretary, Bloomsbury House, 74/77 Great Russell Street, London, WC1B 3DA. Tel.
071-636 7014

  Belfast Newspaper Society
The Secretary, Muir and Addy, Chartered Accountants, 7 Donegall Square West, Belfast,
BT1 6LN. Tel. 26215 (STD code 0232)

Publishers Association
The Secretary, 19 Bedford Square, London, WC1B 3HJ. Tel. 071-580 6321

Reproduction and Graphics Association
The Secretary, 184–186 Old Street, London EC1. Tel. 071-250 0864

Scottish Newspaper Publishers Association
The Secretary, Edinburgh House, 3–11 North St. Andrew Street, Edinburgh EH2 1JU.
Tel. 031-557 3600

Scottish Print Employers Federation
The Secretary, Edinburgh House, 3–11 North St. Andrew Street, Edinburgh, EH2 1JU.
Tel. 031-557 3600

MISCELLANEOUS MANUFACTURING INDUSTRIES

Association of British Reclaimed Rubber Manufacturers
The Secretary, c/o The Rubber Regenerating Company Limited, First Avenue, Trafford
Park, Manchester, M17 1DT. Tel. 061-872 1424

British Button Manufacturers' Association
The Secretary, P.O. Box 3, Berkhamsted, Hertfordshire, HP4 3UG. Tel. Cholesbury 437
(STD code 024-029)

British Jewellery and Giftware Federation Limited
The Secretary, Federation House, 10 Vyse Street, Birmingham B18 6LT. Tel. 021 236
2657

Federation of Master Organ Builders
The Secretary, Petersfield, Hampshire, GU32 3AT. Tel. 0730-62151

Pianoforte Manufacturers' and Distributors Association Limited
The Secretary, Unit 8, Shardlow Business Centre, No 1 Mill, The Wharf, Shardlow,
Derby DE72 2GH. Tel. 0332 792631

CONSTRUCTION

Building (General)

Argyll and District Building Trades Employers Association
The Secretary, 122 Wellington Street, Glasgow G2 2XF. Tel. 041 332 0051

  Orkney Building Trades Federation (Employers)
The Secretary, 154 Union Street, Aberdeen, AB1 1QT. Tel. 23838 (STD code 0224)

  Shetland Building and Allied Trades Association
The Secretary, c/o Pearson and Tawse, Market Street, Lerwick, Shetland. Tel. 120

Building (General) *(continued)*

Building Employers Confederation
  The Secretary, 82 New Cavendish Street, London, W1M 8AD. Tel. *071-580 5588*

Eastern Region
  The Secretary, 95 Tension Road, Cambridge, CB1 2DL. Tel. *355418 (STD code 0223)*

Liverpool Region
  The Secretary, Federation House, Hope Street, Liverpool, L1 9BS. Tel. *051-709 9916*

London Region
  The Secretary, 18-20 Duchess Mews, London, W1N 3AD. Tel. *071-636 38915*

Midland Region
  The Secretary, Federation House, 2309-2311, Coventry Road, Sheldon, Birmingham, B26 3PL. Tel. *021-742 5121*

Northern Counties Region
  The Secretary, Green Lane, Durham, DH1 3JY. Tel. *091-386 1367*

North Western Region
  The Secretary, 2 Conyngham Road, Victoria Park, Manchester, M14 5SH. Tel. *061-224 3214/7*

Southern Region
  The Secretary, Sterling Buildings, Carfax, Horsham, West Sussex, RH12 1DU. Tel. *0403-210256*

South Wales Region
  The Secretary, 66 Cardiff Road, Glan-y-Llyn, Taffs Well, Cardiff, CF4 7YA. Tel. *810661 (STD code 0222)*

South Western Region
  The Secretary, 22 Richmond Hill, Clifton, Bristol, BS8 1BD. Tel. *741161 (STD code 0272)*

Yorkshire Region
  The Secretary, Davidson House, Hales Road, Leeds, LS12 4PW. Tel. *630607 (STD code 0532)*

Clydeside Federation of Community Based Housing Association
  The Secretary, 30 George Square, Glasgow G2 1LH. Tel. *041 221 5562*

Edinburgh and District Master Builders Association
  The Secretary, Craigievar House, 77 Craigmount Brae, Edinburgh EH12 8XF. Tel. *031 339 2477*

Federation of Master Builders
  The Secretary, Gordon Fisher House, 33 John Street, London, WC1N 2BB. Tel. *071-242 7583*

Eastern Region
  (Director) 4 Brooklands Avenue, Cambridge, CB2 2BB. Tel. *Cambridge (0223) 63481*

London Region
  (Director) 19 Station Road, South Norwood, London, SE25 5AH. Tel. *081-771 5451*

Midland Region
  (Director) Mercer House, 780a Hagley Road West, Oldbury, Warley, West Midlands, B68 0PJ. Tel. *Birmingham (021) 421 2241/2.*

Northern Counties and Scotland
  (Director) 4 Hutton Terrace, Newcastle-upon-Tyne, NE2 1QT. Tel. *Tyneside (091) 2813844*

North Western Region
  (Director) 3 Liverpool Road, Birkdale, Southport, Merseyside, PR8 4AR. Tel. *Southport (0704) 68129*

Southern Counties Region
  (Director) 71 London Road, Sevenoaks, Kent, TN13 1AX. Tel. *Sevenoaks (0732) 453050*

South Wales Region
  (Director) 53 Mount Stuart Square, Cardiff, CF1 6DR. Tel. *Cardiff (0222) 464662*

Building (General) *(continued)*

South West Region
> *(Director) 1 St. Paul's Road, Clifton, Bristol, BS8 1LZ.* Tel. *Bristol (0272) 736891.*

Yorkshire Region
> *(Director) 368 York Road, Leeds, LS9 9EB.* Tel. *Leeds (0532) 485122*

Federation of Building and Civil Engineering Contractors (Northern Ireland) Limited
> *The Secretary, 143 Malone Road, Belfast, BT9 6SU.* Tel. *661711 (0232)*

County Armagh Master Builders' Association
> *The Secretary, c/o Rocke, Hall and Company, 52 Bridge Street, Portadown, County Armagh.* Tel. *33326 and 33511*

Ballymena Builders' Association
> *The Secretary, D. Patton and Sons (N.I.) Limited, Ballymoney Road, Ballymena, County Antrim.* Tel. *42141*

Belfast Builders' Association
> *The Secretary, 143 Malone Road, Belfast, BT9 6SU.* Tel. *661711 (0232)*

Fermanagh Master Builders' Association
> *The Secretary, T. Chambers and Sons, 58 Tempo Road, Enniskillen, County Fermanagh.* Tel. *22417*

Larne Builders' Association
> *The Secretary, 27a Station Road, Larne, County Antrim.* Tel. *2409*

Londonderry Master Builders' Association
> *The Secretary, Derry Construction Company Limited, Duncreggan Road, Londonderry.* Tel. *64993*

Newry and District Master Builders' Association
> *The Secretary, 88, Chancellors Road, Dublin Road, Newry, BT35 8LS.* Tel. *Newry 61134/5/6*

North Derry and North Antrim Building Trades Federation
> *Atkinson and Boyd, Chartered Accountants, 24 The Diamond, Coleraine, County Londonderry.* Tel. *3094*

Omagh Construction Employers Association
> *The Secretary, 5 Breezemount Park, Omagh, County Tyrone.* Tel. *2752*

Peterhead Master Builders' Association
> *Alexander and Martins, Solicitors, 1a Longate, Peterhead, Aberdeenshire, AB4 61F.* Tel. *3224*

Scottish Building Employers Federation
> *The Secretary, 13 Woodside Crescent, Glasgow, G3 7UP.* Tel. *041 332 7144*

Aberdeen and District Building Trades Employers Association
> *The Secretary, 154 Union Street, Aberdeen, AB1 1QT.* Tel. *643838 (STD code 0224)*

Eastern Area
> *The Secretary, 60a George Street, Edinburgh, EH2 2LR.* Tel. *031-226 4907*

Forth Valley Building Trades Employers' Association
> *The Secretary, Craigievar House, 77 Craigmount Brae, Edinburgh EH12 8XF.* Tel. *031-339 2477*

Greenock and District Building Trades (Employers) Federation
> *The Secretary, 13 William Street, Greenock, PA15 1BT.* Tel. *Greenock 23341*

Inverness & District Master Builders Association
> *The Secretary, 26 Albyn House, 37A Union Street, Inverness IV1 1QA.* Tel. *237626*

Lochaber Building Employers Association
> *The Secretary, 26 Albyn House, 37A Union Street, Inverness IV1 1QA.* Tel. *0463 237626*

Paisley and District Building Trades Employers Association
> *The Secretary, 122 Wellington Street, Glasgow G2 2XF.* Tel. *041-332 0051*

Perth & District Building Trades Employers Association
> *The Secretary, Albyn House, 37A Union Street, Inverness.* Tel. *Inverness 237626*

Building (General) *(continued)*

Ross-shire Building Trades Employers' Association
> *The Secretary, 26 Albyn House, 37A Union Street, Inverness.* Tel. *237626*

South West Scotland Building Trades (Employers) Association
> *The Secretary, 13 Woodside Crescent, Glasgow G3 7UP.* Tel. *041-332 7144*

Western Isles Building Employers' Association
> *The Secretary, 26 Albyn House, 37A Union Street, Inverness, IV1 1QA.* Tel. *237626*

Civil Engineering

Construction Plant-hire Association
> *The Secretary, 28 Eccleston Street, London, SW1W 9PY.* Tel. *071-730 7117*

Federation of Civil Engineering Contractors
> *The Secretary, Cowdray House, 6 Portugal Street, London, WC2A 2HH.* Tel. *071-404-4020*

Federation of Dredging Contractors
> *The Secretary, 9 Kingsway, London WC2B 6XF* Tel. *071 240 9971*

Gas Conversion Association
> *The Secretary, 235-241 Regent Street, London, W1R 8JU.* Tel. *071-629 2123*

Mastic Asphalt Council and Employers' Federation
> *The Secretary, Lesley House, 6–8 Broadway, Bexley Heath, Kent,* Tel. *081 298 0411*

Representative Organisation of Employers for Local Authorities Services (Building and Civil Engineering)
> *The Secretary, 41 Belgrave Square, London, SW1X 8NZ.* Tel. *071-235 9801*

Specialist Trades

Carpentry and Joinery

Ayshire Master Builders' and Joiners' Association
> *The Secretary, 122 Wellington Street, Glasgow G2 2XF.* Tel. *041-322 0051*

Clydesdale Wrights' and Builders' Employers' Association
> *The Secretary, 13 Woodside Crescent, Glasgow G3 7UP.* Tel. *041-332 7144*

Dumbarton and District Master Wrights' and Builders' Association
> *The Secretary, 122 Wellington Street, Glasgow, G2 2XF.* Tel. *041-332 0051*

Federation of Building Specialist Contractors
> *The Secretary, 82 New Cavendish Street, London W1M 8AD.* Tel. *071 580 5588*

Greenock and District Master Wrights' Association
> *The Secretary, British Linen Bank Buildings, 13 William Street, Greenock, Renfrewshire, PA15 1BY.* Tel. *23341*

Scottish Master Wrights' and Builders' Association
> *The Secretary, 26 West Nile Street, Glasgow, G1 2PQ.* Tel. *041-221 0011*

Painting, Decorating and Glazing

British Decorator's Association
> *The Secretary, 6 Haywra Street, Harrogate, North Yorkshire HG1 5BL.* Tel. *567292 (STD code 0423)*

National Federation of Painting and Decorating Contractors
> *The Secretary, 82 New Cavendish Street, London, W1M 8AD.* Tel. *071-580 5588*

Northern Ireland Master Painters' Association
> *The Secretary, 10 Netherlands Drive, Dunmurry, Belfast, BT17 0EU.* Tel. *778848 or 621091*

Scottish Decorators Federation
> *The Secretary, 41 York Place, Edinburgh.* Tel. *031 557 9345*

Plumbing, Gas Fitting, etc

Aberdeen and District Master Plumbers' Association
> *Alex Stronach & Son and Hunter & Gordon, 12 Carden Place, Aberdeen.* Tel. *53573*

Specialist Trades *(continued)*

Angus and Kincardine Master Plumbers' Association
The Secretary, 5 Taylor Street, Forfar, Tayside Tel. *0307 63294*

Central Counties Plumbing and Mechanical Services
c/o Scott Oswald & Co. C.A. 16 Park Terrace, Stirling, FK8 2JT. Tel. *0786 63336*

Dundee and District Master Plumbers' Association
The Secretary, 34 Reform Street, Dundee, DD1 1RH. Tel. *0382-29222*

Edinburgh, Leith and District Plumbing Employers' Association
The Secretary, 100 High Street, Linlithgow. Tel. *Linlithgow 845144*

Fife and Kinross Master Plumbers' Association
The Secretary, 11 Glenfield Avenue, Cowdenbeath, Fife KY4 9EN. Tel. *0383-510244*

Glasgow and West of Scotland Plumbing Employers' Association
The Secretary, 101 Cumbernauld Road, Stepps, Glasgow, G33 6EP. Tel. *041 779 1774*

Inverness and Northern District Master Plumbers' Association
The Secretary, 17 Queensgate, Inverness, IV1 1DF. Tel. *0463 234288*

Lanarkshire Master Plumbers' Association
c/o Messrs J. B. Soutter Son and Main, 63 Almada Street, Hamilton, Lanarkshire, ML3 0HH. Tel. *0698-286131*

Lancaster, Morecambe and South Lakeland Master Plumbers' Association
The Secretary, 5 Ridge Lane, Lancaster, LA1 1EB.

Moray and Banff Master Plumbers' Association
The Secretary, The Tower, 103 High Street, Elgin, Morayshire. Tel. *542611 (STD code 0343)*

National Association of Plumbing, Heating and Mechanical Services Contractors
(Director and Secretary) Ensign House, Ensign Business Centre, Westwood Way, Coventry, CV4 8JA. Tel. *0203 470626*

NAPH & MSC East Midland Regions
(Regional Director) 13 Newton Road, Leeds, LS7 4DL. Tel. *628100 (STD code 0532)*

NAPH & MSC North Eastern Region
(Regional Director) 13 Newton Road, Leeds, LS7 4DL. Tel. *628100 (STD code 0532)*

NAPH & MSC North Western Region
(Regional Director) Everton House, Wardle Road, Rochdale, Lancashire, OL12 9EN. Tel. *0706-47710*

NAPH & MSC South Eastern Region
(Regional Director) 151-152 Plumstead Road, London, SE18 7DY. Tel. *081-855 7438*

NAPH & MSC South Western Region
(Regional Director)

NAPH & MSC West Midlands Region
(Regional Director) Everton House, Wardle Road, Rochdale, Lancashire, OL12 9EN. Tel. *0706 47710*

Northern Ireland Master Plumbers Association
The Secretary, 16 Donegall Square South, Belfast BT1 5PA. Tel. *0232 321731*

Perth and District Master Plumbers' Association
The Secretary, 14 Dunkeld Road, Perth, PH1 5RW. Tel. *0738 34056*

Scottish and Northern Ireland Plumbing Employers' Federation
The Secretary, 2 Walker Street, Edinburgh, EH3 7LB. Tel. *031-225 2255*

Roofing

Felt Roofing Contractors Employers Association
The Secretary, Fields House, Gower Road, Haywards Heath, West Sussex. RH16 4PL. Tel. *0444-440027*

Flat Roofing Contractors Advisory Board
The Secretary, Maxwelton House, Boltro Road, Haywards Heath, West Sussex, RH16 1BJ. Tel. *0444-440027*

Specialist Trades *(continued)*

Lanarkshire Slaters' and Plasterers' (Employers) Association
The Secretary, 43 Civic Square, Motherwell, ML1 1TP. Tel. *67621 (STD code 0698)*

National Federation of Roofing Contractors
The Secretary, 24 Weymouth Street, London, W1N 3FA. Tel. *071-436-0387*

Scottish Master Slaters' and Roof Tilers Association
The Secretary, 13 Woodside Crescent, Glasgow, G3 7UP. Tel. *041-332 7144*

Miscellaneous Trades

Association of Street Lighting Contractors
The Secretary, 34 Pishiobury Drive, Sawbridgeworth, Herts CM21 0AE. Tel. *0279 722390*

Electrical Contractors' Association Ltd
The Secretary, ESCA House, 34 Palace Court, Bayswater, London, W2 4HY. Tel. *071-229 1266*

Electrical Contractors' Association of Scotland
The Secretary, 23 Heriot Row, Edinburgh, EH3 6EW. Tel. *031-225 7221*

Federation of Brickwork Contractors
The Secretary, Southbank House, Black Prince Road, London, SE1 7SJ. Tel. *071-582 9201*

Federation of Engineering Design Companies Ltd
The Secretary, Broadway House, Tothill Street, London SW1H 9NQ. Tel. *071-222 7777*

Heating and Ventilating Contractors' Association
The Secretary, ESCA House, 34 Palace Court, Bayswater, London W2 4JG. Tel. *071-229-2488*

National Association of Master Masons
The Secretary, Admin House, Market Square (North Side), Leighton Buzzard, Bedfordshire. Tel. *75252*

National Association of Master Masons (Scottish Region)
Adam Ker and Sangster, 90 Mitchell Street, Glasgow, G1 3NW. Tel. *041-221 0424*

National Engineering Construction Employers' Association
The Secretary, Broadway House, Tothill Street, London SW1H 9NQ. Tel. *071 222 7777*

National Federation of Demolition Contractors (Limited by Guarantee)
The Secretary, Cowdray House, 6 Portugal Street, London WC2A 2HH. Tel. *071 404 4020*

National Federation of Terrazzo-Mosaic Specialists *(a)*
The Secretary, First Floor, 251 Brompton Road, London, SW3 2EP. Tel. *071-584 5552*

National Master Tile Fixers' Association
The Secretary, 39 Upper Elmers End Road, Beckenham, Kent, BR3 3QY. Tel. *081 663 0946*

Northern Ireland Insulation Employers' Association
The Secretary, c/o Henry Nelson Ltd., 33–41, Canmore Street, Belfast, BT13. Tel. *41906*

Oil and Chemical Plant Constructors Association
The Secretary, Suites 101–105 (5th Floor) Kent House, 87 Regent Street, London, W1R 7HF. Tel. *071 734 5246*

Refractory Contractors Association
The Secretary, Central House, 32–36 High Street, Stratford, London, E15 2PS. Tel. *081 519 4872*

Society of Industrial Furnace Engineers
The Secretary, Peat. Marwick, Mitchell and Company, P.O. Box 121, 301 Glossop Road, Sheffield, S10 2HN. Tel. *21071*

Scottish Master Plasterers Association
The Secretary, 12 Hill Street, Edinburgh, EH3 3LB. Tel. *031-225 5214*

Thermal Insulation Contractors' Association Limited
The Secretary, Kensway House, 388 High Road, Ilford, Essex IG1 1TC. Tel. *081-514-2120*

DISTRIBUTION, HOTELS, CATERING AND REPAIRS

Wholesale Distribution

Clothing and footwear

Millinery Distributors' Association Ltd.
> *The Secretary, Conway House, 212 Croydon Road. Caterham, Surrey, CR3 6QG.* Tel.
> *43617*

Food and Drink

Aberdeen, Banff and Kincardine Wholesale and Retail Master Butchers' Association
> *The Secretary, Inverurie Scotchmeat, Harlaw Road, Inverurie*

Aberdeen Fish Curers' and Merchants' Association Limited
> *The Secretary, South Esplanade West, Aberdeen AB9 2FJ.* Tel. *0224 897744*

Association of British Abbatoir Owners Limited
> *The Secretary, 5 Charterhouse Square, London EC1M 6EE.* Tel. *071-253 3787*

Birmingham Wholesale Fruit Flower and Potato Merchants' Association
> *The Secretary, Office No. 15, Manor House, Moat Lane, Birmingham B5 5BD.* Tel.
> *021-622 3315*

Covent Garden Tenants' Association Limited
> *The Secretary, A101, Fruit and Vegetable Market, New Covent Garden, London,*
> *SW8 5HH.* Tel. *071-720 7874*

Dairy Trade Federation
> *The Secretary, 19 Cornwall Terrace, London, NW1 4QP.* Tel. *071-486-7244*

Federation of Fresh Meat Wholesalers
> *The Secretary, Harts Corner, London Central Markets, EC1A 9AA.* Tel. *071-236-0346/7*

Glasgow Wholesale Fruit and Vegetable Trades Employers' Association
> *The Secretary, 299 West George Street, Glasgow, G2 4LA.* Tel. *041-221 5951*

London Fish Merchants Association (Billingsgate) Ltd.
> *The Secretary, Office 36, Billingsgate Market, 87 West India Dock Road, London,*
> *E14 8ST.* Tel. *071 515 2655*

Manchester Provision Exchange Limited
> *Birch Littlemore and Company, Chartered Accountants, 110 Washway Road, Sale,*
> *Cheshire, M33 1RF.* Tel. *061-969 5335*

Manchester Meat Salesmen Association
> *The Secretary, c/o Admin Office, City Abbatoir, Riverpark Road, Manchester, M10 6XR.*
> Tel. *061-223-3763 or 3878*

National Association of Wholesale Meat Salesmen of Scotland
> *The Secretary, 65 Renfield Street, Glasgow G2 1NS.* Tel. *041-331-1501*

National Dairymen's Association (Incorporated)
> *The Secretary, 19 Cornwall Terrace, London, NW1 4QP.* Tel. *071-486-7244*

National Federation of Wholesale Grocers and Provision Merchants
> *The Secretary, 18 Fleet Street, London, EC4Y 1AS.* Tel. *071-353 8894*

North of Ireland Wholesale and Export Meat Association
> *The Secretary, c/o Lagan Meat Company, Duncrue Road, Belfast, BT3 9BX.* Tel. *749421*

Scottish Association of Meat Wholesalers
> *The Secretary, 75 Mountgomery Street, Eaglesham, Glasgow.*

Scottish Potato Trade Association
> *The Secretary, 8 Kinnoull Street, Perth.* Tel. *23341 (STD code 0738)*

Smithfield Market Tenants' Association
> *The Secretary, 225 Central Markets, London EC1A 9LH.* Tel. *071-248 3151*

Spitalfields Market Tenants' Association Limited
> *The Secretary, Office 6, Allen House, New Spitalfields Market, 23 Sherrin Road, Leyton*
> *E10 55Q.* Tel. *081 556 1479*

Wholesale Distribution *(continued)*

Stratford Market Tenants' Association Limited
The Secretary, Spitalfields Market, London, E10

Ulster Wholesale Grocers' Association
The Secretary, 10 Arthur Street, Belfast, BT1 4GD. Tel. *23274 and 30888*

West of England and South Wales Provision Trade Association
The Secretary, c/o Alvis Bros. Ltd., Lye Cross Farm, Redhill, Bristol BS18 7RH. Tel. *(0934) 862320*

Western International Market Tenants' Association Ltd.
The Secretary, Office No. 8, Western International Market, Hayes Road, Southall, Middx. Tel. *081-573 5624*

Wholesale Grocers' Association of Scotland
The Secretary, 12 Broughton Place, Edinburgh EH1 3RX. Tel. *031-556-8753*

Paper, Stationery and Books

Association of Newspaper and Magazine Wholesalers, The
3rd Floor, Regent House, 89 Kingsway, London WC2B 6RH. Tel. *071 242 3458*

Federation of London Wholesale Newspaper Distributors
The Secretary, Regent House, 89 Kingsway, London, WC2B 6RH. Tel. *071-242 3458*

National Association of Paper Merchants
The Secretary, 35 New Bridge Street, London, EC4V 6BH. Tel. *071-248 5271*

Sunday Newspaper Distributing Association
The Secretary, Regent House, 89–97 Kingsway, London, WC2B 6RU. Tel. *071-242 3458*

Coal, Builders Materials, Grain and Agricultural Supplies

British Agricultural and Garden Machinery Association Limited
The Secretary, 14–16 Church Street, Rickmansworth, Hertfordshire, WD3 1RQ. Tel. *77241*

Builders' Merchants' Federation
The Secretary, 15 Soho Square, London, W1V 5FB. Tel. *071-439-1753*

Coal Merchants' Federation of Great Britain
The Secretary, Victoria House, Southampton Row, London, WC1B 4DH. Tel. *071-405-0034/5*

Northern Ireland Builders' Merchants Association
The Secretary, 13 Carolsteen Avenue, Helen's Bay, Bangor. Tel. *0247 852869*

Northern Ireland Coal Importers' Association
The Secretary, 8 Castle Lane, Belfast, BT1 5DA. Tel. *41153*

Northern Ireland Plate Glass Association
The Secretary, Room 25, 16 Donegall Square South, Belfast, BT1 5JG. Tel. *0232 321793*

The Scottish Glass Merchants and Glaziers Association
The Secretary, 13 Woodside Crescent, Glasgow, G3 7UP. Tel. *041-332 7144*

United Kingdom Agricultural Supply Trade Association
The Secretary, 3 Whitehall Court, London, SW1A 2EQ. Tel. *071-930 3611*

Timber

British Timber Merchants' Association
The Secretary, Ridgeway House, 6 Ridgeway Road, Long Ashton, Bristol, BS18 9EU. Tel. *0272 394022*

National Sawmilling Association
The Secretary, Clareville House, 26–27 Oxenden Street, London SW1Y 4EL. Tel. *071-839 1891*

East Anglian Sawmilling Association
The Secretary, 24 Bishops Walk, Gunton St. Peter, Lowestoft, NQ32 4JN. Tel. *0502 561515*

Grimsby & Immingham Timber Importers' Association
The Secretary, 28 Dudley Street, Grimsby, South Humberside, DN31 2AB. Tel. *55057*

Wholesale Distribution (continued)

London and District Sawmill Owners' Association
The Secretary, Clareville House, 26–27 Oxendon Street, London, SW1Y 4EL. Tel. 071-839 1891

North West Timber Trade Association
The Secretary, 263a Monton Road, Monton, Eccles, Manchester, M30 9LF. Tel. 061-788 9018

South East Timber Association
The Secretary, 210 Edwin Road, Rainham, Kent, ME8 0JL. Tel. Medway 31546

Northern Ireland Timber Importers' Association
The Secretary, 6 Grey Point, Helen's Bay, Bangor. Tel. 0247 853233

Scrap and Waste Materials

British Scrap Federation
The Secretary, 16 High Street, Brampton, Huntingdon, Cambs., PE18 8TU. Tel. 0480-455249

Ulster Scrap Association
The Secretary, John Eastwood and Sons Limited, Andersons Town Road, Belfast BT11 9AL.

British Secondary Metals Association
The Secretary, Park House, 25 Park Road, Runcorn, Cheshire, WA7 4SS. Tel. 092-85 72400

British Waste Paper Association
The Secretary, Columbia House, 69 Aldwych London WC2B 4DY. Tel. 071-405 9292

Reclamation Association
The Secretary, 16 High Street, Brampton, Huntingdon, Cambs, PE18 8TU. Tel. 55249 (STD code 0480)

Miscellaneous Wholesalers

British Hardware Federation
(Managing-Director) 20 Harbourne Road, Edgbaston, Birmingham, B15 3AB. Tel. 021-454 4385

Coleraine Importers and Exporters' Association
The Secretary, c/o Watts Coal, The Harbour, Coleraine, Co. Londonderry BT52 1BJ. Tel. 0265 2376

The Jute Importers Association
The Secretary, c/o Taybank Works, 60 Arbroath Road, Dundee. Tel. 0382 456504

Retail Distribution

Retail Motor Industry Federation
The Secretary, 201 Great Portland Street, London, W1N 6AB. Tel. 071-580 9122

National Federation of Hide and Skin Markets (Incorporated)
The Secretary, 65 High Street, Great Missenden, Buckinghamshire. Tel. Gt. Missenden 2644

Northern Ireland Wholesale Hardware Merchants Association
The Secretary, 10 Arthur Street, Belfast, BT1 4ED. Tel. 0232 323274

Registered Hide Markets Federation (Northern Ireland) Limited
Miss J. Osborough, 21–25 Windmill Road, Saintfield, Belfast, BT24 7DX. Tel. Saintfield 510–500

Food and Drink

Amalgamated Master Dairymen Ltd
The Secretary, Bradford & Bingley House, 220 Hoe Street, London, E17 3AY. Tel. 081 521 8855

British Independent Grocers' Association
The Secretary, Federation House, 17 Farnborough Street, Farnborough, Hants, GU14 8AG. Tel. 0252-515001/2

Retail Distribution *(continued)*

National Federation of Fishmongers Limited
The Secretary, Queensway House, 2 Queensway, Redhill, Surrey. Tel. *68611*

Northern Ireland Master Butchers' Association
The Secretary, Office 3, Ulster Bank Chambers, 73 May Street, Belfast, BT1 3JL. Tel. *0232 324832*

Retail Confectioners and Tobacconists' Association
The Secretary, Ashley House, 53 Christchurch Avenue, London, N12 0DH. Tel. *081-445 6344*

Retail Fruit Trade Federation Limited
The Secretary, 8–15 Russell Chambers, Covent Garden, London, WC2E 8AB. Tel. *071–836 4137 and 4764*

Scottish Federation of Meat Traders' Associations (Incorporated)
The Secretary, Craigie House, Craigie Knowes Road, Perth PH2 0DQ. Tel. *Perth 37785*

   Glasgow and District Retail Fleshers' Association
The Secretary, 67 Robslee Road, Glasgow, G46 7ER. Tel. *041-638 1774*

Scottish Grocers' Federation
(Director) 29 Alva Street, Edinburgh, EH2 4PS. Tel. *031-225 3214*

Scottish Grocery Trade Employers' Association
The Secretary, 3 Loaning Road, Restalrig, Edinburgh EH7 6JE. Tel. *031 652 2482*

Scottish Milk Trade Federation
The Secretary, Thomson McLintock and Company, Chartered Accountants, 216 West George Street, Glasgow, G2 2PF. Tel. *041-248 5181*

Clothing and Footwear

British Shops and Stores Association
Middleton House, 2 Main Road, Middleton Cheney, Banbury, Oxon OXT1 2TN. Tel. *0295 712277*

Menswear Association of Britain Limited
The Secretary, 19–20 Grosvenor Street, London, W1X 0AS. Tel. *071-491 0076*

Multiple Shoe Retailers' Association
The Secretary, Bedford House, 59–79 Fulham High Street, London. SW6 3JW. Tel. *071 371 5185*

National Shoe Retailer's Council
The Secretary, 9 St. Thomas Street, London, SE1 9SA. Tel. *071-407 5281*

Household Goods

China and Glass Retailers' Association
The Secretary, M16 Victoria House, Vernon Place, London, WC1B 4DA. Tel. *071-404 0520*

National Association of Retail Furnishers
The Secretary, 3 Bernes Street, London, W1P 4JP. Tel. *071-636 1778*

Radio Electrical and Television Retailers' Association (R.T.R.A.) Limited
The Secretary, St. John Terrace, 1 Ampthill St., Bedford, MK4Z 9EY. Tel. *0234 269110*

Scottish House Furnishers' Federation
The Secretary, 203 Pitt Street, Glasgow, G2 4DB. Tel. *041-332 6381*

Wallpaper, Paint and Wallcovering Retailer's Association Limited
The Secretary, 14 Birmingham Road, Walsall, WS1 2NA. Tel. *31134 (STD code 0922)*

Miscellaneous Retailers

Booksellers Association of Great Britain and Ireland
The Secretary, 154 Buckingham Palace Road, London, SW1W 9TZ. Tel. *071-730 8214*

Co-operative Employers Association
The Secretary, Holyoake House, Hanover Street, Manchester, M60 0AS. Tel. *061-832 4300*

Retail Distribution (continued)

National Industrial Relations Executive
> The Secretary, Holyoake House, Hanover Street, Manchester, M60 0AS. Tel.
> 061-832-4300

Sectional Industrial Relations Committees
Midland
> The Secretary, as above

Northern and North Eastern
> The Secretary, as above

North Western
> The Secretary, as above

Southern
> The Secretary, as above

South Western
> The Secretary, P.O. Box 64, Fairfax House, Newgate, Bristol, BS99 7BP. Tel. 297733
> (STD code 0272)

Other Wages Boards
Metropolitan
> The Secretary, as above

Scottish
> The Secretary, as above

British Retailers Association
> The Secretary, Commonwealth House, Second Floor, 1–19 New Oxford Street, London,
> WC1A 1PA. Tel. 071-404-0955

The Consumer Credit Association of the United Kingdom
> The Secretary, 192a Nantwich Road, Crewe, Cheshire, CW2 6BP. Tel. Crewe 213399

The Retail Consortium
> The Secretary, Commonwealth House, 2nd Floor, 1–19 New Oxford Street, London,
> WC1A 1PA. Tel. 071 404 4622

Scottish Retail Credit Association
> The Secretary, 122 Wellington Street, Glasgow, G2 2XG. Tel. 041-332 0070

Federation of Retail Tobacconists
> The Secretary, 546–548 Commercial Road, London, E1 0JE. Tel. 071-790 7411

Federation of Sports Goods Distributors Limited
> The Secretary, 4 Millmead, Dobbins Lane, Wendover, Buckinghamshire, HP22 6BY. Tel.
> 622678 (STD code 0296)

Music Retailers Association
> 24 Fairlawn Grove, Chiswick, London, W4. Tel. 081-994 7592

National Association of Cycle and Motor Cycle Traders Limited
> The Secretary, 31a High Street, Tunbridge Wells, Kent, TN1 1XN. Tel. 26081

National Association of Shopkeepers
> The Secretary, Lynch House, 91 Mansfield Rd., Nottingham, NG1 6LH. Tel. 0602 475046

National Chamber of Trade
> The Secretary, Enterprise House, 59 Castle Street, Reading RG1 7SN. Tel. 0734 566744

National Federation of Retail Newsagents
> The Secretary, Yeoman House, Sekforde Street, Clerkenwell Green, London, EC1R 0HD.
> Tel. 071-253 4225

National Pharmaceutical Association Limited
> The Secretary, Mallinson House, 40-42 St. Peters Street, St. Albans, Herts, AL1 3NP.
> Tel. 0727 32161

Scottish Pharmaceutical Federation
> The Secretary, 135 Buchanan Street, Glasgow, G1 1JG. Tel. 041-221 1235

Retail Distribution *(continued)*

Scottish Tobacco Trade Federation (Retail Confectioners' Association)
The Secretary, 42 Castle Street, Dundee DD2 1JG. Tel. *21374*

Ulster Chemists' Association
The Secretary, 73 University Street, Belfast, BT7 1HL. Tel. *20787*

Hotels and Catering

Belfast and Ulster Licensed Vinters' Association
The Secretary, 26 Bedford Street, Belfast, BT2 7EJ. Tel. *327578 (STD code 0232)*

British Amusement Catering Trades' Association
The Secretary, Bacta House, Regents Wharf, 6 All Saints Street, London, N1 9RQ. Tel. *071 713 7144*

British Hotels, Restaurants and Caterers Association
The Secretary, 13 Cork Street, London, W1X 2BH. Tel. *01-499 6641.* Tel. *73291 (STD code 0532)*

Federation of Retail Licensed Trade Northern Ireland
The Secretary, 91 University Street, Belfast, BT7 1HP. Tel. *0232 327578*

National Federation of Fish Friers Limited
The Secretary, Federation House, 289 Dewsbury Road, Leeds, LS11 5HW. Tel. *73291 (STD code 0532)*

National Union of Licensed Victuallers
The Secretary, Boardman House, 2 Downing Street, Farnham, Surrey, GU9 7NX.

Northern Ireland Hotels and Caterers Association
The Secretary, 108/110 Midland Buildings, Whitla Street, Belfast, BT15 1JP. Tel. *0232 351110*

Scottish Licensed Trade Association
The Secretary, 10 Walker Street, Edinburgh, EH3 7LA. Tel. *031-225 5169*

Repairs

National Association of Multiple Shoe Repairers
The Secretary, 10 Lovvaine Ave, Wickford, Essex, SS12 0DR. Tel. *0702 551566*

Society of Master Shoe Repairers
The Secretary, St. Crispin's House, 21 Station Road, Desborough, Northamptonshire, NN14 2SA. Tel. *Kettering 760374 (STD code 0536)*

TRANSPORT AND COMMUNICATION

Inland Transport (other than rail)

Association of Vehicle Delivery Companies
The Secretary, c/o James Car Deliveries Ltd. 87–89 Foleshill Road, Coventry. Tel. *Coventry 26515*

British Association of Removers Limited
The Secretary, 279 Gray's Inn Road, London, WC1X 8SY. Tel. *071-837 3088*

Coach Operators' Federation
The Secretary, "Rose Vista", 261 Stowey Road, Yatton, Bristol. BS19 4Q. Tel. *0934 832074*

Freight Transport Association Ltd.
The Secretary, Hermes House, 157, St. John's Road, Tunbridge Wells, Kent, TN4 9UZ. Tel. *0892 26171*

Meat Carriers' Association (Southern) Limited
The Secretary, 52 Florence Road, New Cross, London, SE14 6QL. Tel. *081-692 8171*

Morecambe, Heysham and District Coach Owners' Association
The Secretary, 72 West End Road, Morecambe, Lancashire, LA4 4DY. Tel. *410228*

Inland Transport (other than rail) *(continued)*

National Association of Inland Waterway Carriers
> *The Secretary, 9–11 Jameson Street, Hull, HU1 3HR.* Tel. *0482 27281*

Road Haulage Association Limited
> *The Secretary, Roadway House, 104 New Kings Road, London, SW6 4LN.* Tel. *071-736 1183*

Road Transport Association (Northern Ireland)
> *The Secretary, 7 Belvoir Drive, Belfast, BT8 4BA.* Tel. *642829 (STD code 0232)*

Taxi Fleet Operators' Federation
> *(Acting Secretary) 1–3 Brixton Road, London SW9.* Tel. *071-753 7777*

Sea Transport

British Ports Association
> *The Secretary, Commonwealth House, 1-19 New Oxford Street, London WC1A 1DZ.* Tel. *071-242 1200*

British Shipping Federation Limited
> *The Secretary, 30/32 St. Mary Axe, London EC3A 8ET.* Tel. *071-283-2922*

Dundee Shipowners' and Shipbrokers' Association
> *The Secretary, c/o Kinnes Shipping Limited, 21a Commercial Street, Dundee, DD1 3DD.* Tel. *22286/8*

Liverpool Tug Owners' Association
> *The Secretary, c/o Alexandra Towing Co. Ltd., Castle Chambers, 43 Castle Street, Liverpool, L2 9TA.* Tel. *051-227 2151*

Medway Public Wharfingers' Association
> *The Secretary, Offices of the Medway Port Authority, Sheerness Docks, Sheerness, Kent ME12 1RX.* Tel. *0795-580003*

Merseyside Master Boatmen and Dock Pilots' Association
> *The Secretary, North Hornby Dock, Liverpool, L20 1BD.* Tel. *051-933 4333*

Motor Barge Owners' Association
> *The Secretary, 9 Wapping Lane, London, E1 9DA.* Tel. *071-481 3681*

National Association of Port Employers
> *The Secretary, Commonwealth House, 1–19, New Oxford Street, London, WC1A 1DZ.* Tel. *071-242 1200*

GROUP 1

Association of Port Employers for the Medway and Adjacent Ports and Harbours
> *The Secretary, Medway Ports Authority Offices, Sheerness Docks, Sheerness, Kent, ME12 1RX.* Tel. *0795 580003*

Sheerness Port Employers' Association
> *The Secretary, c/o Medway Ports Authority, Dockyard House, Sheerness Docks, Sheerness, Kent, ME12 1RX.* Tel. *0795-580003*

Boston Port Employers' Association
> *The Secretary, Dock Office, Boston Dock, Boston, Lincolnshire.* Tel. *65571 (STD code 0205)*

Great Yarmouth Port Labour Company Limited
> *The Secretary, Steam Mill Lane, Great Yarmouth, Norfolk.* Tel. *55271 (STD code 0493)*

King's Lynn Port Employer's Committee
> *The Secretary, Assistant Docks Manager, British Transport Docks Board, Alexandra Dock, King's Lynn, Norfolk, PE30 2EU.* Tel. *2636 (STD code 0553)*

London Port Employers' Association
> *The Secretary, Central House, 32/66 High Street, Stratford, London, E15 2PS.* Tel *081-519 4872*

Association of Master Lightermen and Barge Owners (Port of London)
> *The Secretary, 69/75 Cannon Street, London EC4N 6AB.* Tel. *071-248 4444*

Sea Transport (continued)

London Enclosed Docks Employers' Association
The Secretary, Central House, 32/66 High Street, Stratford, London, E15 2PS. Tel. *081-519 4872*

London Wharfingers' Association Limited
The Secretary, 69/75 Cannon Street, London, EC4N 6AB. Tel. *071-248 4444*

GROUP 2
Employers Association of the Port of Liverpool
The Secretary, Port of Liverpool Building, Pier Head, Liverpool, L3 1BY. Tel. *051-236 8951*

GROUP 3
National Association of Port Employers (Scottish Group)
The Secretary, c/o Forth Ports Authority, Tower Place, Leith, Edinburgh EH6 7DB. Tel. *031-554 4343*

Greenock Port Employers' Association
The Secretary, 145 Dunlop Street, Greenock, Renfrewshire, PA16 9DB. Tel. *20737 (STD code 0475)*

Inverness Port Labour Employers' Association
The Secretary, c/o McGruther and Marshall Limited, Shore Street, Inverness, IV1 1NT. Tel. *31171 (STD code 0463)*

Kirkwall Port Employers' Association
The Secretary, 3 East Road, Kirkwall, Orkney. Tel. *2804*

Leith Dock Labour Employers' Association
The Secretary, c/o Leith Stevedores Ltd., Tower Place, Leith, Edinburgh, EH6 7DA. Tel. *031-553 1121*

GROUP 4
National Association of Port Employers (South West Group)
The Secretary, Avonmouth Old Dock, Bristol, BS11 9DA. Tel. *Avonmouth 25994 (STD code 0275)*

Bideford Port Employers' Association
The Secretary, c/o M.D. Storage Co. Ltd., 24 The Quay, Bideford, North Devon. Tel. *6006*

East Cornwall Port Employers' Association
The Secretary, E. C. C. Ports Limited, Harbour Office, Par, Cornwall. Tel. *7300*

Bristol Barge Owners' Association
The Secretary, c/o Benjamin Perry and Sons Limited, Junction Cut, Avonmouth Docks, Avonmouth, Bristol, BS11 9DH. Tel. *Avonmouth 4581*

Port of Bristol Master Stevedores' Association
The Secretary, c/o C. J. King and Sons Limited, Avonmouth Docks, Avonmouth, Bristol, BS11 9DH. Tel. *Avonmouth 82511*

Bristol Steamship Owners' Association
The Secretary, P.O. Box 27, Portview Road, Avonmouth, Bristol, BS1 9RH. Tel. *8051*

Port of Bristol Employers' Association
The Secretary, Port Office, St. Andrews Road, Avonmouth, Bristol BS11 9DQ. Tel. *0272 825994*

Port of Gloucester Employers' Association
The Secretary, Dock Office, Sharpness, Berkely, Gloucestershire, G113 9UD. Tel. *Sharpness 644 (STD code 045-384)*

Port of Plymouth Employers' Association
The Secretary, c/o Harbour Office, Guy's Quay, Sutton Harbour, Plymouth, PL4 0ES. Tel. *664186 (STD code 0752)*

South Devon and Dorset Port Employers' Association
The Secretary, Teignmouth Quay Company Limited, Old Quay, Teignmouth, Devon. Tel. *4044 (STD code 062-67), Telex 42745*

Sea Transport *(continued)*

West Cornwall Port Employers' Association
The Secretary, 12 Harbour Terrace, Falmouth, Cornwall. Tel. *313036*

GROUP 5

South Wales Group of the National Association of Port Employers
The Secretary, Port Director's Office, 1–2 Pierhead Building, Cardiff Docks, Cardiff, CF1 5TH. Tel. *471311 (STD code 0222)*

Barry Association of Port Employers
The Secretary, Docks Manager's Office, Barry Docks, Barry, South Glamorgan, CF6 6US. Tel. *732311 Extension 6503 (STD code 044-62)*

Newport (Mon.) Port Employers' Association
The Secretary, Dock Manager's Office, British Transport Docks Board, Alexandra Docks, Newport, Gwent, NPT 2UW. Tel. *244411 (STD code 0633)*

Port of Cardiff Employers' Association
The Secretary, Port Manager's Office, Pierhead Building, Cardiff Docks, Cardiff, CF1 5TA. Tel. *471311 (STD code 0222)*

Swansea Port Employers' Association
The Secretary, Harbour Offices, Adelaide Street, Swansea, SA1 1QR. Tel. *650855 (STD code 0792)*

GROUP 6

Association of Employers of Dock and Riverside Labour at the Port of Goole
The Secretary, c/o BTDB, Stanhope Street, Goole, North Humberside. Tel. *Goole 2691*

Grimsby and Immingham Association of Port Employers
The Secretary, 18 Cleethorpes Road, Grimsby, South Humberside, DN31 3LX. Tel. *0472 353474*

Hull Association of Port Labour Employers
The Secretary, Samman House, Bowlalley Lane, Hull, HU1 1XT. Tel. *0482 24976*

GROUP 7

Port Employers' Association (North East Coast Group)
The Secretary, 1 Bewick Street, Newcastle upon Tyne, NE1 5HS. Tel. *091 2325541*

Port Employers' Association (Tyne and Wear Area)
The Secretary, 1 Bewick Street, Newcastle upon Tyne, NE1 5HS. Tel. *2325541 (STD code 091)*

River Tees Port Employers' Association
The Secretary, Queen's Square, Middlesbrough, Cleveland, TS2 1AH. Tel. *0642-241121.*

Tyne Tug Owners' Association
The Secretary, Mercantile Chambers, Quayside, Newcastle upon Tyne, NE1 3DP. Tel. *22375*

GROUP 8

Southampton Port Employers' Association
Manager, Room 1–14 Dock House, Canute Road, Southampton, SO9 1PZ. Tel. *0703 333806*

Association of Deep Sea Dock Stevedores
The Secretary, c/o Depo Ltd., 31 Dufferin Road, Belfast, BT3 9AA. Tel. *745720*

Belfast Port Employers Association
The Secretary, 63/67 Pilot Street, Belfast, BT1 3AH. Tel. *0232 351148*

Air Transport

Civil Air Transport Employers' Secretariat and National Joint Council for Civil Air Transport
The Secretary, 121 Clare Road, Stanwell, Staines, Middlesex, TW19 7QP. Tel. *Ashford 54034*

Supporting Services

Liverpool United Warehouse Keepers' Conference
The Secretary, P.O. Box 25, Lees Road, Knowsley Industrial Park North, Liverpool

Supporting Services *(continued)*

Merseyside Public Warehousekeepers' Association
The Secretary, Cory Associated Warehouses, Atlantic Industrial Complex, Dunnings Bridge Road, Bootle, Merseyside, L30 4UR. Tel. 051-521 1808

BANKING AND FINANCE

Banking

Association of Indian Banks in the United Kingdom
The Secretary, State Bank of India, State Bank House, 1 Milk Street, London, EC2P 2JP. Tel. 071-600-6444

BUSINESS SERVICES

Association of Midland Advertising Agencies
Association of Northern Advertising Agencies
Association of Scottish Advertising Agencies
The Secretary, 44 Belgrave Square, London SW1X 8QS. Tel. 071-235-7020

PUBLIC ADMINISTRATION

Local Government

Association of County Councils
The Secretary, Eaton House, 66a Eaton Square, London, SW1W 9BH. Tel. 071-235 1200

Association of District Councils
The Secretary, Egginton House, 9 Buckingham Gate, London, SW1E 6LE. Tel. 071-828 7931

Association of District Councils of Northern Ireland
The Secretary, Rural District Council Offices, 2 Church Street, Newtownards, County Down. Tel. 2215

Association of Local Authorities of Northern Ireland
The Secretary, 6 Callendar Street, Belfast, BT1 5BN. Tel. 0232 249286

Association of Metropolitan Authorities
The Secretary, 36 Old Queen Street, London, SW1H 9JE. Tel. 071-222 8100

British Resorts Association
The Secretary, P.O. Box 9, Margate CT9 1XZ. Tel. 0843 25511

Convention of Scottish Local Authorities
The Secretary, 16 Moray Place, Edinburgh, EH3 6BL. Tel. 031-225 1626–7

East Midlands Local Authorities Employers Organisation
The Secretary, West Annexe, County Hall, Glenfield, Leicester LE3 8RN. Tel. 0533 323232

East Midlands Organisation of Local Authorities
(Administration, Professional, Technical and Clerical)
The Secretary, County Hall, Glenfield, Leicester LE3 8RN. Tel. 0533 871313 Ext. 291

   Local Authorities (Manual Employees)
The Secretary

Eastern Provincial Employers Organisation
The Secretary, Third Floor, St. Edmunds House, Lower Baxter Street, Bury St. Edmunds, Suffolk IP33 1ET. Tel. 0284 701285

Essex and Hertfordshire Provincial Employers Organisation
The Secretary, Third Floor, St. Edmunds House, Lower Baxter Street, Bury St. Edmunds, Suffolk IP33 1ET. Tel. 0284 701285

Local Government *(continued)*

Fire Authority for Northern Ireland
> *The Secretary, 43 Castle Street, Lisburn, County Antrim, BT27 4SP. Tel. 4221*

Glasgow Area Federation of Community based Housing Associations
> *The Secretary, 179 West George Street, Glasgow. Tel. 041-221 5562*

Local Authorities Conditions of Service Advisory Board
> *The Secretary, 41 Belgrave Square, London SW1X 8N2. Tel. 071 235 6081*

National Association of Probation Homes and Hostels
> *The Secretary, 78 Stanhope Grove, Beckenham, Kent BR3 3HP. Tel. 081-650 2942*

North Western Local Authorities Employers Organisation
> *The Director, Washington House, New Bailey Street, Manchester M3 5ER. Tel. 061 834 9362*

Northern and North Eastern Provincial Organisation of Employers of Local Authorities Staffs
> *The Secretary, Nelson Street, Gateshead, Tyne and Wear, NE8 1NX. Tel. (091) 4900155*

Representative National Organisation of Employers of New Towns Staff
> *The Secretary, Arndale House, The Arndale Centre, Luton, Bedfordshire, LU1 2TS. Tel. 0582 451166*

South East Employers
> *The Secretary, 33 Staple House, Staple Gardens, Winchester, Hants. SO23 8SR. Tel. 0962 840664*

South Wales Provincial Council for Local Authorities Administrative, Professional, Technical and Clerical Services
> *The Secretary, 79 Eastgate, Cowbridge, South Glamorgan, CF7 7AA. Tel. Cowbridge 2432*

South Wales Provincial Council for Local Authorities Services (Manual Workers)
> *The Secretary, 79 Eastgate, Cowbridge, South Glamorgan, CF7 7AA. Tel. 0446 773848*

The South Western Provincial Employers Association
> *The Secretary, Dennett House, 11 Middle Street, Taunton, Somerset, TA1 1SH. Tel. Taunton 270101*

West Midlands Local Authorities Employers Organisation
> *The Secretary, 4th Floor, Lombard House, 145 Great Charles Street, Queensway, Birmingham B3 3LS. Tel. 021 236 6943*

Yorkshire and Humberside Local Authorities Employers Organisation
> *The Secretary, Arndale House, Arndale Centre, Headingley, Leeds, LS6 2UU. Tel. 787471*

Police

Police Authority for Northern Ireland
> *The Secretary, Fifth Floor, River House, 48 High Street, Belfast, BT1 2DR. Tel. 30111 (STD code 0232)*

MEDICAL AND HEALTH SERVICES

Association of Optical Practitioners
> *The Secretary, 65 Brook Street, London, W1Y 2DT. Tel. 071-629 1091*

British Dental Association
> *The Secretary, 64 Wimpole Street, London, W1M 8AL. Tel. 071-935 0875*

MISCELLANEOUS SERVICES

Educational Services

Polytechnics and Colleges Employers' Forum
> *The Secretary, 7–8 Rathbone Place, London, W1P 1DE. Tel. 071-637 3336*

Recreational and Cultural Services

Art Studios Photographic Laboratories Association
The Secretary, Elizabeth House, 76 Longbridge Road, Barking. Essex, IG11 8SF. Tel. *081-594-3052*

Association of British Orchestras
The Secretary, Francis House, Francis Street, London SW1P 1DE. Tel. *071-828 6913*

Association of Post Production Companies
The Secretary, 4 D'Arblay Street, London W1V 3FD. Tel. *071 734 8335.*

Cinema Exhibitors' Association
The Secretary, Royalty House, 72 Dean Street, London, W1V 5HB. Tel. *071-734 9551*

Advertising Film and Videotape Producers' Association
The Secretary, 26 Noel Street, London, W1. Tel. *071-434 2651*

British Film and Television Producers' Association Ltd
The Secretary, Paramount House, 162–170 Wardour Street, London W1V 4LA. Tel. *071 437 7700*

Football League Limited
The Secretary, 319 Clifton Drive South, Lytham St. Annes, Lancashire, FY8 1JG. Tel. *0253 729421*

Independent Programme Producers' Association
The Secretary, 50/51 Berwick St., London W1A 4RD. Tel. *071 439 7034*

Kinematograph Renters' Society Limited
The Secretary, Royalty House, 72-73 Dean Street, London, W1V 5HB. Tel. *071-437 4383*

Music Retailers Association Limited
The Secretary, 24 Fairlawn Grove, London W4 5EX. Tel. *081-994 7592*

National Trainers' Association
The Secretary, 42 Portman Square, London, W1H 0AP. Tel. *071-935-2055*

Northern Ireland Turf Guardians' Association
The Secretary, 10 Pottinger's Entry, Belfast, BT1 4DT. Tel. *32960 (STD code 0232)*

Scottish Theatrical Proprietors and Managers Association
The Secretary, 27 Maxwell Drive, Glasgow, G74 4HH. Tel. *East Kilbride 20749*

Showmen's Guild of Great Britain
The Secretary, Guild House, 41 Clarence Street, Staines, Middlesex, TW18 4SY. Tel. *0784 461805/6*

Test and County Cricket Board
The Secretary, Lords Cricket Ground, London, NW8 8QZ. Tel. *071 286 4405*

Theatres' National Committee
The Secretary, Gloucester House, 19 Charing Cross Road, London, WC2H 0ES. Tel. *071-839 5107*

Association of Circus Proprietors of Great Britain
The Secretary, Mellor House, Primrose Lane, Mellor, Blackburn, Lancs. BB1 92N. Tel. *0254-661621*

Association of Touring and Producing Managers
The Secretary, Suite 41-43, 18 Charing Cross Road, London, WC2H 0HR. Tel. *071-836 2133 and 2341*

Theatrical Management Association Ltd.
The Secretary, Bedford Chambers, The Piazza, Covent Garden, London, WC2E 8HQ. Tel. *071-836 0971*

West End Theatre Managers Ltd.
The Secretary, Bedford Chambers, The Piazza, Covent Garden, London, WC2E 8HQ. Tel. *071-836 0971*

Personal Services

Association of British Laundry, Cleaning and Rental Services Limited
The Secretary, 7 Churchill Court, 58 Station Road, Harrow, Middlesex HA2 7SA. Tel. *081-863 7755*

Personal Services *(continued)*

Incorporated Guild of Hairdressers, Wigmakers and Perfumers
The Secretary, Syndicate House, 27–29 Westgage, Barnsley S70 2DJ. Tel. 0226 297083

Laundry Industrial Relations Committee of the Co-operative Employers Association, Co-operative Union Limited
The Secretary, Holyoake House, Hanover Street, Manchester, M60 0AS. Tel. 061-834 4300

London Association of Funeral Directors
The Secretary, 146A High Street, Tonbridge, Kent. TN9 1BB. Tel. 0732 770332

National Federation of Master Window Cleaners and General Cleaners
The Secretary, Summerfield House, Harrogate Road, Reddish, Stockport, Cheshire, SK5 6HH. Tel. 061-432 8754

National Hairdressers' Federation
The Secretary, 11 Goldington Road, Bedford, MK40 3JY. Tel. 60332 (STD code 0234)

Proprietary Crematoria Association
The Secretary, The Lodge, Hartington Road, Brighton, BN2 3PL. Tel. 61601 (STD code 0273)

Society of Master Shoe Repairers Limited
The Secretary, St Crispins House, 21 Station Road, Desborough, Northants, NN14 2SA. Tel. 0536 760374

Swansea and District Hairdressers Association
The Secretary, 55 Wind Street, Swansea

Ulster Launderers' Association
The Secretary, c/o Lilliput (Dunmurry) Ltd., Dunmurry, Belfast, BT17 7AP. Tel. 618353 (STD code 0232)

NATIONAL ORGANISATIONS COVERING VARIOUS INDUSTRIES

Confederation of British Industry
(Director-General)
(Secretary) Centre Point, 103 New Oxford Street, London WC1A 104. Tel. 071-379 7400
Director (N.I.) Fanum House, 108 Great Victoria Street, Belfast, BT2 7PD. Tel. 0232 226658

Isle of Man Employers' Federation
The Secretary, G.P.O. Box 12, Kensington House, Rosemount, Douglas, Isle of Man. Tel. 3206 (STD code 0624)

Londonderry Employers' Federation Limited
The Secretary, Court Chambers, 250 Bishop Street, Londonderry. BT48 6PR. Tel. 263131 (STD code 0504)

National Association of Industries for the Blind and Disabled, Incorporated
The Secretary, Triton House, 43a High Street South, Dunstable, Bedfordshire, LU6 3RZ. Tel. 66796 (STD code 0582)

Wages Councils (Employers') Consultative Committee
21 Tothill Street, London, SW1H 9LP. Tel. 071-930 6711

Trade Union Federations, Trade Unions and Other Employees' Associations

Contents

Trade Union Federations, Trade Unions and Other Employees' Associations

So far as is possible the following list of Trade Unions, Trade Union Federations and other Employees' Associations is confined to those organisations (whether permanent or temporary) which either:

(*a*) consist wholly or mainly of workers of one more descriptions and are organisations whose principal purposes include the regulation of relations between workers of that description or those descriptions and employers or employers' associations; or

(*b*) consist wholly or mainly of—

(i) constituent or affiliated organisations which fulfil the conditions specified in paragraph (*a*) above (or themselves consist wholly or mainly of constituent or affiliated organisations which fulfil those conditions), or

(ii) representatives of such constituent or affiliated organisations;

and in either case are organisations whose principal purposes include the regulation of relations between workers and employers or between workers and employers' associations, or include the regulation of relations between their constituent or affiliated organisations.

AGRICULTURE, FORESTRY, FISHING

Agriculture

Association of Somerset Inseminators
The Secretary, 12 Woodborough Road, Winscombe, Avon. Tel. Winscombe 3211

National Farmers' Union Headquarters Staff Association
The Secretary, 22 Long Acre, London, WC2E 9LY. Tel. 071 235 5077

Fishing

Lough Neagh Fishermen's Association
The Secretary, 10A High Street, Antrim. Tel. 63301 (STD code 0238 41)

Ulster Sea Fishermen's Association
Captain the Rt. Hon. W. J. Long, J.P., 12 Hamilton Road, Bangor, County Down, BT20 4LE. Tel. Bangor 2766

ENERGY AND WATER SUPPLY

Coal Mining

British Association of Colliery Management
The Secretary, B.A.C.M. House, 317 Nottingham Road, Old Basford, Nottingham, NG7 7DP. Tel. Nottingham 785819 and 786949 (STD code 0602)

National Association of Colliery Overmen, Deputies and Shotfirers
The Secretary, Simpson House, 48 Netherhall Road, Doncaster, DN1 2PZ. Tel. 0302 84813

Cannock Chase Area
The Secretary, 30 Station Road, Hednesford, Staffordshire, WS12 4DL. Tel. 2860

Durham Area
The Secretary, John Street, Durham, DH1 4DE. Tel. Durham 091 38 47400

Kent Area
The Secretary, c/o 37 Channel Lea, Walmer, Deal, Kent, CT14 7VG. Tel. 0304 362024

Leicestershire Area
The Secretary, 15 Hotel Street, Coalville, Leicester, LE6 2EQ. Tel. 36836 (STD code 0530)

Midland Area
The Secretary, Falcon House, 15 Pelham Road, Nottingham. Tel. 607278 (STD code 0602)

Coal Mining *(continued)*

North Staffordshire Area
The Secretary, 3 Albert Street, Newcastle-under-Lyme, Staffordshire, ST5 1JP. Tel.
610670

North Western Area
The Secretary, 4 Upper Dicconson Street, Wigan, WN1 2AD. Tel. *42008 (STD code
0942)*

Northumberland Area
The Secretary, Quayside, Blyth, Northumberland, NE24 3AL. Tel. *(0670) 352747*

Yorkshire Area
The Secretary, Deputy House, 37 Church Street, Barnsley, South Yorkshire, S70 2AR. Tel.
0226 203743

Scottish Area
The Secretary, 19 Cadzow Street, Hamilton, Lanarkshire, ML3 6EE. Tel. *284981 (STD
code 0698)*

South Wales Area
The Secretary, 70 Neville Street, Cardiff, CF1 8LS. Tel. *21853 (STD code 0222)*

National Union of Mineworkers
The Secretary, Holly Street, Sheffield S1 2GT. Tel. *0742 766900*

Ashton & Haydock Branch
The Secretary, 9 Lord Street, Eccleston, Chorley, Lancs. Tel. *Eccleston 451061*

Billinge Branch
The Secretary, 21 Canberra Road, Marsh Green, Wigan, Lancs. Tel. *0942 212238*

Cannock, Chase and Pelshall District, Midland Area
The Secretary, Miners Officers, 47 Station Road, Hednesford, Stafford. Tel. *045 382112*

Cokemen's Area
The Secretary, 17 Victoria Road, Barnsley, South Yorkshire. Tel. *0226 283146*

Colliery Officials' and Staffs' Area Region No. 1
The Secretary, 14a Bond Street, Wakefield, West Yorkshire, WF1 2QD. Tel. *363228/9*

Colliery Officials' and Staffs' Area, Region No. 2
The Secretary, 11 Chequer Road, Hyde Park, Doncaster, South Yorkshire, DN1 2AA. Tel.
0302 349679

Colliery Officials' and Staffs' Area, Region No. 3
The Secretary, 88 Bradford Street, Bolton, Lancashire. Tel. *0204 21296*

Colliery Officials' and Staffs' Area, Region No. 4
The Secretary, 58 Station Road, Sutton-in-Ashfield, Nottingham, NG17 5GA. Tel. *0623
599444*

Derbyshire Area
The Secretary, Miners' Offices, 98/100 Saltergate, Chesterfield, Derbyshire. Tel. *0246
211091*

Durham Area
The Secretary, Red Hill, Durham, DH1 4BB. Tel. *3515*

Durham Engineering Group No. 1 Area
The Secretary, 17 Hallgarth Street, Durham, DH4 6NP. Tel. *091 336 4828*

Durham Mechanics Group No. 1 Area
The Secretary, 26 The Avenue, Durham DH1 4ED. Tel. *091 3861375*

Leicester Area
The Secretary, Miner's Offices, Bakewell Street, Coalville, Leicestershire. Tel. *0530
32085*

Midland Area
The Secretary, Winton House, Stoke Road, Shelton, Stoke on Trent. Tel. *0782 744026*

North Stafford Federation Midland Area
*The Secretary, Miner's Office, Park Road, Burslem, Stoke-on-Trent, Staffordshire,
ST6 1SG.* Tel. *0782 837093*

Coal Mining *(continued)*

North Wales Area
The Secretary, Miners' Offices, Bradley Road, Wrexham, Clwyd. Tel. *94 265638*

North Western Area
The Secretary, Miners' Office, Bridgeman Place, Bolton, Lancashire, BL2 1DL. Tel. *0204 21680*

North Western Area—Clifton Branch
The Secretary, Agecroft Colliery, Pendlebury, Swinton, Manchester. Tel. *061 736 5312*

North Western Area—E & B Winders
The Secretary, 369 St. Helens Road, Leigh, Lancs, WN7 3PK. Tel. *0942 601396*

North Western Area—E & B North Wales Branch
The Secretary, 37 Sandway Road, Wrexham, North Wales, LL11 2RB. Tel. *0978 357039*

North Western Area—Parkside Branch
The Secretary, Parkside Colliery, Newton le Willows, Merseyside.

North Western Area—Parsonage Branch
The Secretary, Parsonage Colliery, Clifton Street, Leigh, Lancs. Tel. *0942 671315.*

North Western Area—Pendlebury Branch
The Secretary, Top Temple Drive, Swinton, Manchester. Tel. *061–736 5312 Ext. 236*

North Western Area—Plank Lane Branch
The Secretary, Bickershaw Colliery, Leigh. Tel. *0942 261050*

North Western Area—St. Helens Craftsmens' Branch
The Secretary, 16 Goodleigh Place, Sutton Leach, St. Helens, WA9 4NL. Tel. *0744 817446*

North Western Area—Sutton Manor Branch
The Secretary, 79 Canberra Avenue, Castle Heath, St. Helens, Merseyside, WA9 5RS.

Northern Colliery Officials and Staffs Association
The Secretary, Trafalgar House, Carliol Square, Newcastle-upon-Tyne, NE1 6UQ. Tel. *2327969*

Northumberland Area
The Secretary, Burt Hall, Northumberland Road, Newcastle-upon-Tyne, NE1 8LD. Tel. *091 2327351*

Northumberland Mechanics Group No. 1 Area
The Secretary, Burt Hall, Northumberland Road, Newcastle on Tyne.

Power Group Area
The Secretary, 9 Birch Terrace, Hanley, Stoke-on-Trent, ST1 4HL. Tel. *0782–262759*

Pride of Golborne Miners' Lodge Trade Union and Checkweigh Fund
The Secretary, Golborne Colliery, Golborne, Warrington. Tel. *Wigan 725765*

South Staffordshire, East Worcestershire and Shropshire Districts
The Secretary, 31 Queen Street, Wolverhampton WV1 3JW

South Wales Area
The Secretary, Woodlands Terrace, Maesycoed, Pontypridd, Mid Glamorgan CF37 1DZ. Tel. *(0446) 404092*

Warwickshire District Midland Area
The Secretary, Miners' Offices, Bulkington Road, Bedworth, Nuneaton. Tel. *Bedworth 313181*

Yorkshire Area
The Secretary, 2 Huddersfield Road, Barnsley, South Yorkshire, S70 2LS. Tel. *284006*

Yorkshire Colliery Enginemen, Firemen and Allied Trades Association Group 1 (Craftsmen) Area
The Secretary, Chancery Chambers, Commercial Street, Castleford, West Yorkshire

Scottish Area
The Secretary, 5 Hillside Crescent, Edinburgh EH7 5DZ. Tel. *031 556 2323*

Coal Mining *(continued)*

Scottish Colliery Enginemen, Boilermen and Tradesmen's Association
The Secretary, 5 Hillside Crescent, Edinburgh EH7 5DZ. Tel. 031 556 2323

Union of Democratic Mineworkers
The Secretary, The Sycamores, Moor Road, Bestwood, Nottingham, NG6 8UE. Tel. 0602 763468

Clerical and Supervisory Staff
The Secretary, The Sycamores, Moor Road, Bestwood, Nottingham, NG6 8UE. Tel. 0602 755077

Colliery Trades and Allied Workers Section
The Secretary, 5/7 Refuge Buildings, St. Thomas Street, Sunderland, SR1 1BL. Tel. 091 510 9021

Nottingham Section
The Secretary, Miners Offices, Berry Hill Lane, Mansfield, Notts., NG18 4JU. Tel. 0623 26094

South Derbyshire Section
The Secretary, Miners Offices, Alexandra Road, Swadlincote, Burton on Trent DE11 9AZ. 0283 221200

Electricity

Engineers' and Managers' Association
The Secretary, Flaxman House, Gogmore Lane, Chertsey, Surrey, KT16 9JS Tel. 0932 564131

Electrical Power Engineers Association
The Secretary, Flaxman House, Gogmore Lane, Chertsey, Surrey, KT16 9JS Tel. 0932 564131

Gas

Gas Higher Management Association
The Secretary, Epic House (5.2A), Charles Street, Leicester, LE1 3SH. Tel. 0533 539071

Nuclear Fuel

Springfields Foremans Association
The Secretary, 22 Conder Green Road, Ashton on Ribble, Preston, PR2 1PE. Tel. 0772 734226

Oil

Offshore Industry Liaison Committee
The Secretary, Criterion Buildings, 52 Guild Street, Aberdeen, AB1 2NB. Tel. 0224 210118.

METAL MANUFACTURE

Associated Metalworkers' Union
The Secretary, 92 Worsley Road North, Worsley, Manchester, M28 5QW. Tel. 0204 793245

Dexion Staff Association
The Secretary, Dexion-Comino International Ltd., Maylands Avenue, Hemel Hempstead, Herts., HP2 7EW. Tel. Hemel Hempstead 42261

Iron and Steel Trades Confederation
The Secretary, Swinton House, 324 Gray's Inn Road, London, WC1X 8DD. Tel. 071–837 6691

Joint Committee of Light Metal Trades Unions
The Secretary, Imperial Buildings, Corporation Street, Rotherham, South Yorkshire, S60 1PB. Tel. 382820 (STD code 0709)

Metal Manufacture *(continued)*

National Craftsmen's Co-ordinating Committee (Iron and Steel Industry)
The Secretary, Hayes Court, West Common Road, Bromley, Kent

National Union of Domestic Appliances and General Operatives
*The Secretary, Imperial Buildings, Corporation Street, Rotherham, South Yorkshire, S60
1PB Tel: 382820 (STD code 0709)*

Star Aluminium Managerial Staff Association
*The Secretary, Bishop Percy's House, Cartway, Bridgnorth, Shropshire, WV16 4BC. Tel.
3298*

Union of Dexion Workers
*The Secretary, Dexion-Comino International Ltd., Maylands Avenue, Hemel Hempstead,
Herts HP2 7EW. Tel. 0442 42261 Ext. 210*

MANUFACTURE OF NON METALLIC MINERAL PRODUCTS

Cement

Independent Union of Owner Operators
*The Secretary, Creg-na-baa, Ironbridge Road, Madeley, Telford, Shropshire. Tel. 0952
581485*

Glass and Ceramic Goods

Ceramic and Allied Trades Union
*The Secretary, Hillcrest House, Garth Street, Hanley, Stoke-on-Trent, ST1 2AB. Tel.
Stoke-on-Trent 272755 (STD code 0782)*

National Union of Flint Glassworkers
The Secretary, 43 Dennis Hall Road, Amblecote, Stourbridge, West Midlands.

Pressed Glassmakers' Society of Great Britain
The Secretary, 14 Trevethick Street, Gateshead, Tyne and Wear.

CHEMICAL INDUSTRY

Central Committee of I.C.I. Foremen's and Supervisors' Associations
*The Secretary, Engineering Works Construction, I.C.I. Mond Division, Westonpoint, P.O.
Box 18, Runcorn, Cheshire. Tel. 73434*

National Unilever Managers' Association
*The Secretary, New Street Chambers, 67a New Street, Birmingham, B2 4DU. Tel.
021–643 4431*

Whatman PLC Staff Association
*The Secretary, c/o Whatman International Ltd, Whatman House, St. Leonard's Road,
20/20 Maidstone, Kent. MS16 0LS. Tel. 0622 676670.*

METAL GOODS, ENGINEERING AND VEHICLES

Vehicles, Aircraft and Aerospace

Association of HSDE (Hatfield) Employees
The Secretary, "Sunnyview", Causeway Close, Potters Bar, Hertfordshire, EN6 5MW

The Association of Licensed Aircraft Engineers (1981)
*The Secretary, The Old Court House, London Road, Ascot, Berks, SL5 7EN. Tel. 0990
26138*

British Aerospace plc Senior Staff Association
The Secretary, 130 Gloucester Road North, Bristol, BS12 7BQ.

Vehicles, Aircraft and Aerospace *(continued)*

British Aerospace plc
The Secretary, Site B, Argyle Way, Stevenage, Herts. Tel. *31345*

Rediffusion Simulation Staff Association
The Secretary, c/o Rediffusion Simulation Ltd., Gatwick Road, Manor Royal, Crawley, W. Sussex. Tel. *28811*

Space and Communications (Stevenage) Staff Association
The Secretary, 47 Passingham Avenue, Hitchin, Herts. Tel. *0462 50760*

Miscellaneous Engineering Production

Amalgamated Engineering and Electrical Union
The Secretary, 110 Peckham Road, London SE15 5EL. Tel. *071 703 4231*

Card Dressers' Society
The Secretary, 20, Eleventh Avenue, Liversedge, West Yorkshire, Tel. *879037*

Card Setting Machine Tenters' Society
The Secretary, 36 Greenton Avenue, Scholes, Cleckheaton, West Yorkshire, BD19 6DT. Tel. *Bradford 670022 (STD code 0274)*

Confederation of Shipbuilding and Engineering Unions
The Secretary, 140–142 Walworth Road, London, SE17 1JW. Tel. *071-703 2215*

Costain Engineering Senior Staff Association
The Secretary, Petrocarbon House, Sharston Road, Wythenshawe, Manchester M22 4TB. Tel. *061 998 7000*

Engineering Craft Association
The Secretary, 116 Bordesley Green East, Birmingham, B9 5SJ. Tel. *021 784 7926*

Engineering and Fasteners Trade Union
The Secretary, 42 Galton Road, Warley, Worc's. Tel. *021 429 2594*

Johnson Matthey plc Headquarters Staff Society
The Secretary, 43 Hatton Garden, London, EC1. Tel. *071-430 0011*

Jones and Shipman Administrative Staff Association
The Secretary, c/o Jones and Shipman, Narborough Road South, Leicester, LE3 2LF. Tel. *0533 896222*

National Union of Lock and Metal Workers
The Secretary, Bellamy House, Wilkes Street, Willenhall, West Midlands, WV13 2BS. Tel. *66651 (STD code 0902)*

National Union of Scalemakers
The Secretary, Queensway House, 57 Livery Street, Birmingham, B3 1HA. Tel. *021-236 8998*

Sheffield Wool Shear Workers' Trade Union
The Secretary, 50 Bankfield Road, Sheffield, S6 4RD. Tel. *Sheffield 333688*

The Shipbuilding Engineering and Aerospace Group
The Secretary, Station House, Fox Lane North, Chertsey, Surrey, KT16 9HW. Tel. *0932 564131*

Society of Shuttlemakers
The Secretary, 211 Burnley Road, Colne, Lancs, BB8 8JD. Tel. *0282 866716*

Thorne E.M.I. Electronics Ltd. (Feltham) Junior and Middle Management Staff Association
The Secretary, 16 Springfield Road, Ashford, Middlesex TW15 2LR. Tel. *0784 250838*

Wire Workers Union
The Secretary, Prospect House, Alma Street, Sheffield, S3 8SA. Tel. *721674 (STD code 0742)*

FOOD, DRINK

Brewing and Malting

Guinness Brewing Staff Association (U.K.)
The Secretary, Park Royal Brewery, London, NW10 7RR. Tel. 081-965 7700

Guinness Park Royal Supervisors Association
The Secretary, Park Royal Brewery, Park Royal, London, NW10 7RR. Tel. 081-965 7700

Miscellaneous Food and Drink

Bakers' Food and Allied Workers' Union
The Secretary, Stanborough House, Great North Road, Stanborough, Welwyn Garden City, Hertfordshire, AL8 7TA. Tel. 07072 60150

Cadbury Schweppes Representative Association
The Secretary, 11 Mallings Avenue, Astley

Cadbury Schweppes Senior Managers' Association
The Secretary, Pera, Bryher, Isles of Scilly, Cornwall TR23 0PR. Tel. 0720 22325

Colman Association of Staff
The Secretary, Colman Foods, Carrow, Norwich, NR1 2DD. Tel. 0603 672574

TEXTILES

Woollen and Worsted

Bradford and District Power Loom Overlookers' Society
The Secretary, Inveresk House, 31 Houghton Place, Bradford, BD1 3RG. Tel. 0274 727966

Halifax and District Power Loom Overlookers' Society
The Secretary, 57 Savile Park Street, Halifax, West Yorkshire, HX1 3EG. Tel. 66238 (STD code 0422)

Huddersfield and Dewsbury Power Loom Overlookers' Society
The Secretary, Dewsbury Club and Institute, Dewsbury, Huddersfield, W. Yorkshire. Tel. 468744

Huddersfield and District Carding Engineers Association
The Secretary, 77 Prospect Road, Longwood, Huddersfield, HD3 4UY. Tel. Huddersfield 55899 (STD code 0484)

Keighley and District Power Loom Overlookers' Society
The Secretary, 26 Prospect Mount, Fell Lane, Keighley, West Yorkshire, BD22 6LS. Tel. 607758

Leeds and District Power Loom Overlookers' Society
The Secretary, 21 Carlton Avenue, Pudsey, West Yorkshire, LS28 7LR. Tel. 0532 572944

National Federation of Carding Engineers' Association
The Secretary, 77 Prospect Road, Longwood, Huddersfield, HD3 4UY. Tel. Huddersfield 55899 (STD code 0484)

Pattern Weavers Society
The Secretary, 38 St. Pauls Road, Kirkheaton, Huddersfield. Tel. 0484-24988

Yorkshire Association of Power Loom Overlookers
The Secretary, 20 Hallfield Road, Bradford, BD1 3RQ. Tel. 0274-727966

Hosiery and Knitted Goods

National Union of Hosiery and Knitwear Workers
The Secretary, 55 New Walk, Leicester, LE1 7EB. Tel. 556703 (STD code 0533)

Carpets

Halifax and District Carpet Power Loom Tuners' Association
The Secretary, 3 City Lane, Wheatley, Halifax, West Yorkshire. Tel. 59710

Carpets *(continued)*

National Affiliation of Carpet Trade Unions
> *The Secretary, Carpet Weavers' Hall, Callows Lane, Kidderminster, Worcestershire, DY10 2JG.* Tel. *3192 (STD code 0562)*

Northern Carpet Trades Union
> *The Secretary, 22 Clare Road, Halifax, West Yorkshire, HX1 2HX.* Tel. *60492 (STD code 0422)*

Power Loom Carpet Weavers' and Textile Workers' Union
> *The Secretary, Carpet Weavers' Hall, Callows Lane, Kidderminster, Worcestershire, DY10 2JG.* Tel. *823192 (STD code 0562)*

Scottish Carpet Workers' Union
> *The Secretary, 27 Cook Street, Glasgow, G5 8JN.* Tel. *041 429 5199*

Cotton and Other Textiles

Loom Overlookers

Blackburn and District Amalgamated Power Loom Overlookers' Association
> *The Secretary, Overlookers' Offices, 9 Wellington Street, St. John's, Blackburn, BB1 8AF.* Tel. *Blackburn 51760 (STD code 0254)*

Church and Oswaldtwistle Power Loom Overlookers' Society
> *The Secretary, 140 Exchange Street, Accrington, Lancs.* Tel. *(0254) 393073*

Colne and District Power Loom Overlookers' Association
> *The Secretary, 2 Knowsley Street, Colne, Lancashire, BB8 0SD.* Tel. *863021 (STD code 028 24)*

Derby Powerloom Overlookers' Association
> *The Secretary, 141 Alvaston Street, Alvaston, Derby.* Tel. *0332 2961*

General Union of Associations of Loom Overlookers
> *The President, 9, Wellington Street, St. John's, Blackburn, BB1 8AF.* Tel. *0254 51760*

Haslingden and District Powerloom Overlookers' Society
> *The Secretary, 15 North Street, Haslingden, Rossendale, Lancashire.* Tel. *0706 217362*

Hyde and District Loom Overlookers' Association
> *The Secretary, 14 George Street, Denton, Manchester, M34 3DJ.* Tel. *061-320 0501*

National Association of Power Loom Overlookers
> *The Secretary, 4 Alder Close, Moss Side, Leyland, Preston, Lancs PR5 3TT.* Tel. *0772 453033*

Nelson and District Power Loom Overlookers' Society
> *The Secretary, Overlookers' Society, Jude Street, Nelson, Lancashire, BB9 7NP.* Tel. *Nelson 64066 (STD code 0282)*

Oldham Association of Loom Overlookers
> *The Secretary, 4 Milford Avenue, Hollins, Oldham, Lancashire, OL8 3UP.* Tel. *682-6138*

Skipton and District Power Loom Overlookers' Association
> *The Secretary, 139 Colne Road, Earby, Colne, Lancashire, BB8 6XU.* Tel. *0282 843471*

United Association of Power Loom Overlookers
> *The Secretary, 130 Drake Street, Rochdale, Lancashire, OL16 1PN.* Tel. *46448 (STD code 0706)*

Tape Sizers

Accrington, Church and Oswaldtwistle Tape Sizers' Friendly Protective Society
> *The Secretary, 64 Westwood Street, Accrington, Lancashire, BB5 4BL.* Tel. *381503*

Lancashire Amalgamated Tape Sizer's Association
> *The Secretary, 2A New Brown Street, Nelson, Lancashire, BB9 7NY.* Tel. *0282 64055*

Amalgamated Tape Sizers' Friendly Protection Society
> *The Secretary, 34 Southfield Road, Holcombe Brook, Bury, Lancs.* Tel. *0204 883391*

Cotton and Other Textiles *(continued)*

Association of Preparatory Workers
> *The Secretary, 2a New Brown Street, Nelson, Lancashire, BB9 7NY.* Tel. *64055 (STD code 0282)*

Blackburn and District Tape Sizers' Society
> *The Secretary, 8 Moorside Avenue, Blackburn, BB1 2BA.* Tel. *Blackburn 53813*

Bolton Tape Sizers' Protective Society
> *The Secretary, 172 Paulham Street, Bolton, BL3 3DX.* Tel. *62154 (STD code 0204)*

Burnley and District Tape Sizers' Protective Society
> *The Secretary, 27 Emily Street, Burnley, BB11 2HR.* Tel. *24614 (STD code 0282)*

Weavers, Winders and Warpers

Amalgamated Society of Textile Workers and Kindred Trades
> *The Secretary, "Foxlowe", Market Place, Leek, Staffordshire, ST13 6AD.* Tel. *382068 (STD code 0538)*

Burnley, Nelson, Rossendale and District Textile Workers' Union
> *The Secretary, 33 Carr Road, Nelson, Lancs. BB9 7JS*

Oldham and District Weavers', Winders', etc., Association
> *The Secretary, Weavers' Institute, Bartlam Place, Horsedge Street, Oldham, Lancashire, OL1 3SU.* Tel. *061-624 4439*

Padiham and District Weavers', Winders' and Warpers' Association
> *The Secretary, M.M., Weavers' Institute, Sowerby Street, Padiham, Burnley, Lancashire, BB12 8DB.* Tel. *Padiham 71531 (STD code 0282)*

General Textiles and Other Trades

Amalgamated Association of Beamers, Twisters and Drawers (Hand and Machine)
> *The Secretary, 27 Every Street, Nelson, Lancashire, BB9 7NE.* Tel. *64181 (STD code 0282)*

Amalgamated Textile Warehouse Operatives
> *The Secretary, Colne and District Branch, 4 Hall Street, Colne, Lancs. BB8 0DJ.* Tel. *Colne 863419*
> *The Secretary, Padiham Branch, 165 Halifax Road, Brierfield, Lancs. BB9 5BL.* Tel. *0282 694616*

Bengal Trade Union Congress (International)
> *The Secretary, Alexander Johnson (Solicitors), 384 Bethnal Green Road, London E2 0AH*

British Federation of Textile Technicians
> *The Secretary, 14 George St., Denton, Manchester, M34 3DJ.* Tel. *061-320 0501*

Guild of Textile Supervisors
> *The Secretary, 20 Redacre Road, Gorton, Manchester, M18 8RD.* Tel. *061 223 2577*

Hosiery and Textile Dyers' and Auxiliary Association
> *The Secretary, 70 Westfield Road, Hinckley, Leicestershire, LE10 1AP.* Tel. *38592 (STD code 0455)*

  Bradford No. 3 Branch
> *The Secretary, Hayhurst House, Preston Street, Bradford, West Yorkshire, BD7 1JE*

Nelson and District Clothlookers and Warehouse Association
> *The Secretary, 165 Halifax Road, Brierfield, Nelson, Lancs, BB9 5BL.* Tel. *0282 694616*

Northern Counties Textile Trades Federation
> *The Secretary, 2A New Brown Street, Nelson, Lancs, BB9 7NY.* Tel. *0282 64055*

North Lancashire & Cumbria Textile Workers Association
> *The Secretary, 6 Sedgwick Street, Preston, PR1 1TP.* Tel. *53415 (STD code 0772)*

Nottingham and District Dyers' and Bleachers' Association
> *The Secretary, 59 Bannerman Road, Bulwell, Nottingham, NG6 9JA.* Tel. *273007*

General Textiles and Other Trades *(continued)*

Scottish Union of Powerloom Technicians
The Secretary, 3 Napier Terrace, Dundee DD2 2SL. Tel. 0382-612196

Textile Manufacturing Trades Federation of Bolton and Surrounding Districts
Miss H. P. Unsworth, J.P., 77 St. George's Road, Bolton. Tel. 22726

FOOTWEAR AND CLOTHING

Footwear

National Union of the Footwear, Leather and Allied Trades
*The Secretary, The Grange, 108 Northampton Road, Earls Barton, Northampton,
NN6 0JH. Tel. Northampton 810326 (STD code 0604)*

Rossendale Union of Boot, Shoe and Slipper Operatives
*The Secretary, "Taylor House", 7 Tenterfield Street, Waterfoot, Rossendale, Lancashire,
BB4 7BA. Tel. 0706 215657*

Clothing, Hats and Gloves

London Society of Tie Cutters
The Secretary, 5 Whitelands Close, Wickford, Essex, SS11 7EW. Tel. 0268 762215

TIMBER AND FURNITURE

Furniture, Timber and Allied Trades' Union
*The Secretary, "Fairfields", Roe Green, Kingsbury, London, NW9 0PT. Tel. 081-204
0273*

Lancashire Box, Packing Case and General Woodworkers' Society
The Secretary, 50 Burton Road, Withington, Manchester, M20 9EB. Tel. 061-434 6650

National Federation of Furniture Trade Unions
*The Secretary, "Fairfields", Roe Green, Kingsbury, London, NW9 0PT. Tel. 081-204
0273*

PAPER, PRINTING AND PUBLISHING

Paper

Craftsmen's National Negotiating Committee (Papermaking and Boardmaking Industry)
(Convenor) L. K. Dixon, 110 Peckham Road, London, SE15 5EL. Tel. 071-703 4231

Printing and Publishing

Graphical, Paper and Media Union
The Secretary, 63–67 Bromham Road, Bedford. MK40 2AG. Tel. 0234 351521)

Institute of Journalists
*The Secretary, C. Underwood, 2 Dock Offices, Surrey Quays, Lower Road, London. SE16
2XL. Tel. 071-252 1187*

National Union of Journalists
*The Secretary, Acorn House, 314–320 Gray's Inn Road, London, WC1X 8DP. Tel.
071-278 7916*

Printing Trades Alliance
*The Secretary, Holroyde House, 53 Addington Square, London, SE5 7LB. Tel. 071-701
1950*

Staff Association of the Printing and Publishing Industry Training Board
The Secretary, Merit House, Edgware Road, London, NW9 5AG. Tel. 081-205-0162

MISCELLANEOUS MANUFACTURING INDUSTRIES

Association of Plastic Operatives and Engineers
The Secretary, c/o Hunter Plastics Ltd, Natham Way, Woolwich, SE28 Tel. 081 855 9851

Military and Orchestral Musical Instrument Makers' Trade Society
The Secretary, 2 Whitehouse Avenue, Borehamwood, Herts WD6 5EF

Teston Independent Society of Cricket Ball Makers
*The Secretary, 197 Tonbridge Road, Wateringbury, Maidstone, Kent ME18 5NY. Tel.
0622 813638*

CONSTRUCTION

Balfour Beatty Staff Association
The Secretary, 7 Mayday Road, Thornton Heath, Surrey, CR4 7XA. Tel. 081-684 6922

Building Trades Union
The Secretary, 1 Cecil Avenue, Wembley, Middlesex

Construction Industry Training Board Staff Association
The Secretary, Bircham Newton, Kings Lynn, Norfolk, PE31 6RH. Tel. 0553 776677

Howard Doris Staff Association
The Secretary, Loch Kishorn Construction Site, Wester Ross

A. Monk and Company Staff Association
The Secretary, c/o Ridgeway, 19–21 Palmyra Square, Warrington. Tel. 0925 54221

National House Building Council Staff Association
*The Secretary, 55 Rokeby Crescent, Strathaven, Strathclyde, ML10 6EG. Tel. (0357)
21816*

Self Employed and Employed Electricians
The Secretary, 1 Fulbrook Close, Embrook, Wokingham, Berks. Tel. 0734 786753.

Union of Construction, Allied Trades and Technicians
*The Secretary, Ucatt House, 177 Abbeville Road, Clapham, London, SW4 9RL. Tel.
071-622 2362*

DISTRIBUTION, HOTELS, CATERING AND REPAIRS

Wholesale and Retail Distribution

The Bread Salesmens Trade Union
The Secretary, 102 High Street, Belfast BT1 2BG

Cadbury Schweppes Representatives Association
*The Secretary, 11 Malling Avenue, Broughton, Astley, Leicester, LE9 6QS.. Tel. 0455
283203*

Harrods Staff Union
*The Secretary, c/o Harrods Limited, Knightsbridge, London, SW1. Tel. 071-730 1234
Ext. 2604*

National Association of Co-operative Officials
*The Secretary, Saxone House, 56 Market Street, Manchester, M1 1PW. Tel.
061-834 6029*

Retail Book, Stationery and Allied Trades Employees' Association
The Secretary, 8/9 Commercial Road, Swindon, SN1 5RB. Tel. 0793 615811

Rowntree Mackintosh Sales Staff Association
The Secretary, 25 Bolney Drive Eastwood, Essex, SS9 5HQ. Tel. 0702 528372

Rumbelows Branch Managers Association
The Secretary, 29 Marsby Way, Stockport, Cheshire. Tel. 061 480 5245.

Wholesale and Retail Distribution *(continued)*

Rumbelows Retail Staff Association
> *The Secretary, 21 Tiverton Avenue, North Shields, Tyne & Wear NE29 8PZ*

Union of Shop, Distributive and Allied Workers
> *The Secretary, Oakley, 188 Wilmslow Road, Fallowfield, Manchester, M14 6LJ.* Tel.
> *061-224 2804*

Hotels and Catering

Birmingham Union of Club Stewards
> *The Secretary, 2 Saxon Way, Chelmsley Wood, Birmingham, B37 5AY.* Tel. *021-770 9440*

National Association of Licensed House Managers
> *The Secretary, 9 Coombe Lane, Raynes Park, London, SW20 8NE.* Tel. *01-947 3080*

National Union of Club Stewards
> *The Secretary, King Edward VII Hotel, High Street, Tibshelf, Derby.* Tel. *0773 87 3234*

Nottingham and District Federation of Club Stewards
> *The Secretary, Bentinck Miners Welfare, Kirkby in Ashfield, Nottingham.* Tel. *0632*
> *752284*

Rank Hotels Staff Association
> *The Secretary, 42 Gondar Gardens, London NW6 1HG.*

TRANSPORT AND COMMUNICATION

Railways

Associated Society of Locomotive Engineers and Firemen
> *The Secretary, 9 Arkwright Road, Hampstead, London, NW3 6AB.* Tel. *071-431 0275*

British Transport Police Force Federation
> *The Secretary, Room 89, 2nd Floor, Victoria House, Temple Gate, Bristol, BS1 6PW.* Tel.
> *211327 (STD code 0272)*

Federation of Professional Railway Staff
> *The Secretary, 99 Friar Gate, Derby, DE1 1EZ.* Tel. *021 771 3215*

International Transport Workers Federation
> *The Secretary, 133/135 Great Suffolk Street, London SE1 1PD.* Tel. *071-403 2733*

National Union of Rail, Maritime and Transport Workers
> *Unity House, Euston Road, NW1 2BL.* Tel. *071 387 4771*

Transport Salaried Staffs Association
> *The Secretary, "Walkden House", 10 Melton Street, Euston, London, NW1 2EJ.* Tel.
> *071-387 2101*

Other Inland Transport

National Owner Drivers' Association, U.K.
> *The Secretary, 12 Broad Green, Wellingborough, Northants.* Tel. *0933 76384*

North-East Coast Tug-Boatmen's Asociation
> *The Secretary, 6 Burnett Close, Wallsend NE28 9AJ*

United Road Transport Union
> *The Secretary, 76 High Lane, Chorlton-cum-Hardy, Manchester, M21 1FD.* Tel. *061-881*
> *6245*

Sea Transport

British Seafarers' Joint Council
> *(Joint Secretaries) Merchant Navy and Airline Officers' Association, "Oceanair House",*
> *750–760 High Road, Leytonstone, E11 3BB.* Tel. *01-989 6677*

Sea Transport *(continued)*

National Union of Seamen, Maritime House, Old Town, Clapham, London, SW4 0PJ.
Tel. *071-622 5581*

The European Ferryman's Association (Dover)
The Secretary, 11 Diamond Terrace, Greenwich, London. SE10

Humberside Port Workers Union
The Secretary, 15 Lime Tree Avenue, Garden Village, Hull, HU8 8QB. Tel. *0482 75526*

Master Mates Engineers Administration Union
The Secretary, 45 St. Katherines Way, St Katherines by the Tower, London E1 9LB.

National Union of Marine, Aviation and Shipping Transport Officers
The Secretary, "Oceanair House", 750–760 High Road, Leytonstone, London, E11 3BB.
Tel. *081-989 6677*

National Union of Rail, Maritime and Transport Workers
The Secretary, Unity House, Euston Road, NW1 2BL. Tel. *071 387 4771*

Officers' (Merchant Navy) Federation Limited
The Secretary, "Oceanair House", 750-760 High Road, Leytonstone, E11 3BB. Tel.
081-989 6677

United Kingdom Pilots' Association
The Secretary, (Oxon.), 20 Peel Street, London, W8 7PD. Tel. *071-727 1844*

Air Transport

Air 2000 Flight Crew Association
The Secretary, Fermain Cottage, Browns Lane, Wilmslow, Cheshire.

British Air Line Pilots Association
The Secretary, 81 New Road, Harlington, Hayes, Middlesex, UB3 5BG. Tel. *081-759
9331*

British Airlines Stewards and Stewardesses Association 1989
The Secretary, New Road, Harlington, Middx.

Gatwick Handling Staff Association
The Secretary, Gatwick Airport, Gatwick, West Sussex, RH6 0QU. Tel. *0293 502580*

Lufthansa Staff Association United Kingdom
The Secretary, 12 Montrose Avenue, Whitton, Middlesex, TW2 6HS. Tel. *081-894 1329*

Professional Flight Instructors' Association
*The Secretary, c/o Post Office, CSE Aviation Ltd, Oxford Airport, Kidlington, Oxon,
OX5 1RA.* Tel. *0865 841234 Ext 332*

Supporting Services

Airport Fire Fighters Federation
The Secretary, BAA Fire Centre, Building 450, Heathrow Airport, Hounslow, Middlesex.
Tel. *081-897 3535*

Humberside Portworkers
The Secretary, 15 Lime Tree Avenue, Garden Village, Hull. Tel. *0482 75526*

Postal and Telecommunications

British Telecommunication Union Committee
The Secretary, 14–15 Bridewater Square, London E2. Tel. *071-379 6662*

Communication Managers Association
The Secretary, Hughes House, Ruscombe Road, Twyford, Reading, Berks RG10 9JD. Tel.
0734 342300

Engineering Officers' Technical Association
The Secretary, 9–11 Kensington High Street, London W8 5NP. Tel. *081-644 8444*

Postal and Telecommunications *(continued)*

National Communications Union (Engineering and Clerical Group)
The Secretary, Greystoke House, 150 Brunswick Road, Ealing, London W5 1AW. Tel.
081-988 2981

National Federation of Sub-Postmasters
The Secretary, Evelyn House, 22 Windlesham Gardens, Shoreham-by-Sea, West Sussex,
BN4 5AZ. Tel. 0273 452324

Post Office Senior Staff Negotiating Council
The Secretary, Society of Civil and Public Servants, 124–126 Southwark Street, London,
SE1 0TU. Tel. 071-928 9671

Post Office Union's Council
The Secretary, Room 121, Empire House, St. Martin's-le-Grand, London EC1. Tel.
071-606 6486

Society of Telecom Executives
1 Park Road, Teddington, Middlesex, TW11 0AR. Tel. 081 943 5181

Union of Communication Workers
The Secretary, U.C.W. House, Crescent Lane, Clapham Common, London, SW4 9RN.
Tel. 071-622 9977

BANKING AND FINANCE

Banking

Abbey National Staff Association
The Secretary, ANSA House, 15B Mile End Road, Colchester, Essex, CO4 5BT. Tel. 0206
577545

Banking, Insurance and Finance Union
The Secretary, Sheffield House, 1B Amity Grove, Raynes Park, SW20 0LG. Tel. 081-946
9151

Building Staff Association (Bank of England)
The Secretary, Bank of England, Threadneedle Street, London EC2R 8AH. Tel. 071-601
4444 Ext. 3452

Barclays Group Staff Union
The Secretary, Oathall House, Oathall Road, Haywards Heath, West Sussex, RH16 3DG.
Tel. 458811 (STD code 0444)

Lloyds Bank Group Staff Union
The Secretary, Jansel House, 648 Hitchen Road, Luton, Beds. Tel. 0582 25433

Nat West Staff Association
The Secretary, 8–10 Dean Park Crescent, Bournemouth, Dorset, BH1 1HH. Tel. 0202
293616

Commercial Bank of Australia (London) Staff Association
The Secretary, 12 Old Jewry, London, EC2R 8DP. Tel. 071-600 8761

Girobank Senior Managers Staff Association
The Secretary, Girobank plc, Bridle Road, Bootle, Merseyside, G1R 0AA. Tel. 051 966
2163

Hong Kong Bank Group U.K. Staff Association
The Secretary, 99 Bishopsgate, London EC2P 2LA. Tel. 071-638 2366

Societe Generale Staff Association
The Secretary, 60 Gracechurch Street, London. Tel. 071-626 4236

Staff Association of Bank of Baroda (European Operations)
The Secretary, 31–32 King Street, London EC2V 8EN. Tel. 071 606 8888

Other Financial Institutions

Alliance & Leicester Building Society Staff Association
The Secretary, Hove Administration Centre, Hove Park, Hove, East Sussex, BN3 7AZ.
Tel. 0273 775454

Other Financial Institutions *(continued)*

Bradford and Bingley Building Society Staff Association
The Secretary, 16/17 The Shambles, Malton, N. Yorks YO17 0LZ. Tel. 0653 697634

Britannia Building Society Staff Association
The Secretary, 249 Leek Road, Endon, Stoke-on-Trent, Staffs, ST9 9BJ. Tel. 05382 504073

Cheshire Building Society Staff Association
The Secretary, Castle Street, Macclesfield, Cheshire. Tel. 0625 613612 Ext. 2200

Cheshire and Northwich Staff Association
The Secretary, 23 The Mall, Sale, Cheshire M33.

Derbyshire Building Society Staff Association
The Secretary, P. O. Box 1, Room 4, 1 Duffield Hall, Duffield, Derby DE5 1AG. Tel. Derby 841791

Dunfermline Building Society Staff Association
The Secretary, 12 East Port, Dunfermline, Fife.

Halifax Building Society Staff Association
The Secretary, 46 Old Bath Road, Charvil, Reading. Tel. 0734 341808

Heart of England Building Society Staff Association
The Secretary, Olympus Avenue, Tachbrook Park, Leamington Spa Tel. 0926 496111

Leeds and Holbeck Building Society Staff Association
The Secretary, Holbeck House, 105 Albion Street, Leeds LS1 5AS. Tel. 0532 459511

Leeds Permanent Building Society Staff Association
The Secretary, 239 Stainbeck Lane, Leeds, LS7 2PN

National and Provincial Building Society Staff
The Secretary, Hennymoore House, 11 Manor Row, Bradford. Tel. 0274 394703

Nationwide Group Staff Association
The Secretary, Middleton Farmhouse, 37 Main Road, Middleton Chevy, Banbury, Oxfordshire, OX17 2QT. Tel. 0295 710767

Portman Building Society Staff Association
The Secretary, Portman House, Richmond Hill, Bournemouth. Tel. 0202 292444

Scarborough Building Society Staff Association (SOCASS)
The Secretary, P.O. Box 6, Scarborough, North Yorkshire, YO12 6EQ. Tel. 0723 368155

Skipton Building Society Staff Assocation
The Secretary, c/o 59 High Street, Skipton, Yorks, Tel. 0756 4581

Staffordshire Building Society Staff Association
The Secretary, 21a Worcester Street, Wolverhampton WV2 4LD. Tel. (0902) 713314

West Bromwich Building Society Staff Association
The Secretary, 321 High Street, West Bromwich. Tel. 021 525 3411

Woolwich Independent Staff Association
The Secretary, 45 High Street, Bexley, Kent DA5 1AB. Tel. 0322-56712

Yorkshire Building Society Staff Association
The Secretary, 173 Taylor Street, Batley, West Yorkshire, WF17 5AY. Tel. 0274 734822 Ext 4469

INSURANCE

Australian Mutual Provident Society Staff Association
The Secretary, A.M.P. House, Dingwall Road, Croydon, Surrey, CR9 2AP. Tel. 081-686 5611

Britannic Field Staff Association
Joint Secretries, 114 Emscote Road, Warwick, CV34 5QJ. Tel. 0926 496858

Insurance *(continued)*

Clerical, Medical and General Staff Association
   The Secretary, Narrow Plain, Bristol, BS2 0JH. Tel. 0272 278013

Commercial Union Group Managers' Association
   The Secretary, St. Helens, 1 Undershaft, London EC3P 3DQ. Tel. 071-283 7500

Commercial Union Group Staff Association
   The Secretary, 13 Bushey Close, Kenley, Surrey CR2 5AT. Tel. 081-668 7196

Confederation of Insurance Trade Unions
   The Secretary, Tranpsort House, Smith Square, London, SW1P 3JB. Tel. 071-828 7788

Friends Provident Line Managers' Association
   *The Secretary, Friends Provident Life Office, Pixham Lane, Dorking, Surrey, RH4 1QA.
   Tel. 0306 740123*

Ideal Field Staff Association
   The Secretary, 227 Coton Road, Nuneaton. Tel. 342878

Legal and General Senior Managers Association
   The Secretary, Temple Court, 11 Queen Victoria Street, London EC4. Tel. 071-248 9678

Lloyd's Register (U.K.) Staff Association
   The Secretary, 71 Fenchurch Street, London, EC3M 4BS. Tel. 071-709 9166

Managerial Staff Association of the Provincial Insurance Group of Companies
   *The Secretary, Provincial Insurance Co. Ltd., Stramongate, Kendal, Cumbria LA9 4BE.
   Tel. 0539 23415*

National Union of Insurance Workers
   The Secretary, 27 Old Gloucester Street, London, WC1N 3AF. Tel. 071-405 6798/1083

Sun Alliance Managers Association
   *The Secretary, Sun Alliance and London Insurance Group, 1 Bartholomew Lane, London
   EC2. Tel. 0403 214678*

Sun Alliance Staff Union
   The Secretary, c/o 1 Bartholomew Lane, London EC3N 2AB. Tel. 071-588 2345

Sun Life Staff Association
   The Secretary, 11/16 Dighton Street, Bristol BS2 8DL. Tel. 0272 426911

United Friendly Agents' Association
   The Secretary, 37 Litton Way, Leeds, LS14 2DL. Tel. 0532 734712

United Friendly Head Office Management Association
   *The Secretary, 42 Southwark Bridge Road, London SE1 9HE. Tel. 071 928 5644 Ext.
   251*

Scottish Equitable Staff Association
   The Secretary, 28 St. Andrew Square, Edinburgh, EH2 1YF. Tel. 031-556 9101 Ext. 250

PUBLIC ADMINISTRATION

National Government

Association of First Division Civil Servants
   The Secretary, 2 Caxton Street, London SW1H 0QH. Tel. 071-222 6242

Association of Her Majesty's Inspectors of Taxes
   The Secretary, 2 Caxton Street, London, SW1H 0QH.

Association of Magisterial Officers
   The Secretary, 35 High Street, Crawley, West Sussex, RH10 1BQ. Tel. 0293 547515

Audit Commission Staff Association
   *The Secretary, District Auditors Office, 7th Floor Chesham House, Sheffield, S1 4HR.
   Tel. 0742 720619*

National Government *(continued)*

Civil and Public Services Association
The Secretary, 160 Falcon Road, London, SW11 2LN. Tel. 071-924 2727

Council of Civil Service Unions
The Secretary, 58 Rochester Row, London, SW1P 1JU. Tel. 071-834 8393

Diplomatic Service Association
*The Secretary, Room K322, Foreign and Commonwealth Office, King Charles Street,
London SW1A 2AH. Tel. 071-270 2766*

Government Communication Staff Federation
The Secretary, Room A, 0904A, Priors Road, Cheltenham, Glos. Tel. 0242 573906

Immigration Service Union
The Secretary, 12 Church Street, Harwich, Essex. Tel. 0255 553039

Inland Revenue Staff Federation
*The Secretary, Douglas Houghton House, 231 Vauxhall Bridge Road, London
SW1V 1EH. Tel. 071-834 8254*

Institution of Professional Civil Servants
The Secretary, 75–79 York Road, London SE1 7AQ. Tel. 071-928 9951

Isle of Man Government Officers' Association
*The Secretary, Room I, 31 Central Government Offices, Back's Road, Douglas, Isle of
Man. Tel. (0624) 26262 Ext. 20318*

Ministry of Defence Staff Association (MODSA)
*The Secretary, Unit 3, Old Malt House, Springfield Road, Grantham, Lincs. Tel. 0476
79528*

National Union of Civil and Public Servants
The Secretary, 124–130 Southwark Street, London, SE1 0TU. Tel. 071-928 9671

Northern Ireland Public Service Alliance
*The Secretary, Harkin House, 54 Wellington Park, Belfast, BT9 6BZ. Tel. 661831 (STD
code 0232)*

Health and Social Service Boards Division
Address as above

Civil Service Professional Officers Association
As above

Civil Service Association
As above

Public Officers Division
As above

Prison Governors Association
Room 134 Horseferry House, Dean Ryle Street, London. Tel. 071 217 8591

Prison Officers' Association
*The Secretary, Cronin House, 245 Church Street, Edmonton, London, N9 9HW. Tel. 081
803 0255*

The Prison Service Union
The Secretary, 47 Great Innings South, Watton-at-Stone, Hertford

Retired Officers' Association
*The Secretary, c/o G1 Branch, H.Q. London District, Chelsea Bks, Chelsea Bridge Rd,
London. Tel. 071 414 3233*

Procurators Fiscal Society
The Secretary, Procurator Fiscal's Office, Sheriff Court, Cupar, Fife. Tel. 4991

Scottish Prison Officers' Association
The Secretary, 21 Calder Road, Edinburgh, EH11 3PF. Tel. 031-443 8105

Local Government

Association of Local Authority Chief Executives
The Secretary, City Hall, Bradford, BD1 1HY. Tel. 0274 652001

Local Government *(continued)*

Association of Principal Fire Officers
The Secretary, 1 Lancaster Circus, Queensway, Birmingham B4 7DJ. Tel. *021 300 6700*

Association of Public Service Finance Officers
The Secretary, Terminus House, The High, Harlow, Essex, CM20 1TZ. Tel. *434444 (STD
code 0279)*

Association of Registrars of Scotland
The Secretary, 45 Ardrossan Road, Saltcoats, KA21 5BS

Association of Scottish Local Government Directors of Personnel
The Secretary, Falkirk District Council, Municipal Bldgs., Falkirk. Tel. *0324 24911 Ext.
2233*

Belfast City Council Senior Staff Association
The Secretary, Gas Department, Tower Buildings, Ormeau Avenue, Belfast, BT2 8HW.
Tel. *20261 Ext. 33 (STD code 0232)*

Corporation of London Staff Association
The Secretary, The Porch, Guildhall, London EC2 2EJ. Tel. *606-3030 Ext. 1482*

County Surveyors' Staff Association (Hampshire)
The Secretary, The Castle, Winchester, Hampshire, SO23 8UD. Tel. *0962 841841*

Federated Union of Managerial and Professional Officers
The Secretary, Terminus House, The High, Harlow, Essex. CM20 1TZ. Tel. *0279 434444*

Fire Brigades' Union
The Secretary, Bradley House, 68 Coombe Road, Kingston upon Thames, Surrey. Tel.
081-541 1765

Greater London Senior Staff Guild
The Secretary, Room 158 North Block, County Hall, London SE1 7PB. Tel. *071-633
6727*

Guild of County Land Agents and Valuers
The Secretary, Estates Office, County Hall, Taunton, Somerset. Tel. *Taunton (0823)
55373*

National Association of Fire Officers
The Secretary, 10 Cuthbert Road, Croydon, Surrey, CR0 3RB. Tel. *081-686 8863*

National and Local Government Officers Association
The Secretary, Nalgo House, 1 Mabledon Place, London, WC1H 9AJ. Tel. *071-388 2366*

National Union of Public Employees
The Secretary, Civic House, 20 Grand Depot Road, Woolwich, London SE18 6SF. Tel.
081-854 2244

New Towns Chief Officers' Association
*The Secretary, Peterborough Development Corporation, P.O. Box 3, Stuart House,
Peterborough.* Tel. *68931 (STD code 0733)*

Retained Firefighters' Union
The Secretary, Firefighter House, 1 Woodville Road, Maidstone, Kent, ME15 7BS. Tel.
0622 762455

Scottish Association of Amenity Supervisory Staff
The Secretary, 27 Allen Avenue, Deanpark, Renfrew. Tel. *041 886 6039*

Scottish Society of Directors of Planning
The Secretary, Lothian Regional Council, 1 Parliament Square, Edinburgh, EH1 1TU.
Tel. *031-226 6131*

Society of Local Council Clerks
The Secretary, P.O. Box 2, Council Offices, Newton Aycliffe, Co. Durham. Tel.
0325-300700

Society of Registration Officers (Births, Deaths and Marriages)
The Secretary, The Register Office, Royal York Buildings, Old Steine, Brighton. Tel. *0273
722795*

Local Government *(continued)*

Society of Union Employees (NUPE)
> *The Secretary, c/o NUPE, Blackgates House, Bradford Road, Tingley, Wakefield
> WF3 1SD.* Tel. *0532 537654*

Police

Association of Chief Police Officers of England, Wales and Northern Ireland
> *The Secretary, A.C.P.O. Office, New Scotland Yard, Broadway, London, SW1H 0BG.* Tel.
> *01-230 2456*

Association of Chief Police Officers (Scotland)
> *Chief Constable The Secretary, Lothian and Borders Police Headquarters, Fettes
> Avenue, Edinburgh, EH4 1R3.* Tel. *031-311 3131*

Association of Scottish Police Superintendents
> *Chief Superintendent The Secretary, Lothian and Border Police, 'A' Divisional
> Headquarters, Causewayside, Edinburgh.* Tel. *031 667 3361*

Police Federation of England and Wales
> *The Secretary, 15–17 Langley Road, Surbiton, Surrey, KT6 6LP.* Tel. *01-399 2224*

Police Federation for Northern Ireland
> *The Secretary, Garnerville, Old Holywood Road, Belfast BT4 2NX.* Tel. *0232 760831*

Police Superintendents' Association of England and Wales
> *Chief Superintendent The Secretary, 209–211 High Road, Chiswick, W4 2DR.* Tel.
> *01-994 1254*

Scottish Police Federation
> *The Secretary, 5 Woodside Place, Glasgow G3 7PD.* Tel. *041-332 6268*

Superindents' Association of Northern Ireland
> *Chief Superintendent W. J. Gray, Royal Ulster Constabulary, Station, Portadown, Co.
> Armagh.* Tel. *086-10-32424*

EDUCATION

Association of Agricultural Education Staffs
> *The Secretary, Kirkley Hall College, Ponteland, Newcastle Upon Tyne, NE20 0AQ.* Tel.
> *0661 860808*

Association of Cambridge University Assistants
> *The Secretary, 55 Trumpington Street, Cambridge, CB2 1RG.* Tel. *67425 (STD code
> 0223)*

Association of Career Teachers
> *The Secretary, Hillsboro, Castledine Street, Loughborough, Leicestershire.* Tel. *214617
> (STD code 0509)*

Association of Educational Psychologists
> *The Secretary, 3 Sunderland Road, Durham, DH1 2LH.* Tel. *091-384 6392*

Association of Teachers and Lecturers
> *The Secretary, Gordon House, 7 Northumberland St. London WC2N 5DA.* Tel. *071-930
> 6441*

Association of University and College Lecturers
> *The Secretary, 104 Albert Road, Southsea, Hampshire PO5 2SN.* Tel. *0705 818625*

Association of Principals of Colleges
> *The Secretary, 12 Fir Close, Poynton, Stockport, Cheshire.* Tel. *0625 859413*

Association of Teachers of Domestic Science
> *The Secretary, Hamilton House, Mabledon Place, London, WC1H 9BJ.* Tel. *071-387
> 1441*

Association of University Teachers
> *The Secretary, United House, 1 Pembridge Road, London, W11 3HJ.* Tel. *071-221 4370*

Education *(continued)*

Association of Vice Principals of Colleges
The Secretary, City of Liverpool Community College, Riversdale Rd, Aigburth, Liverpool L19 3QR. Tel. *051 494 2539*

British Association of Advisers and Lecturers in Physical Education
The Secretary, Kingsmill & Co Solicitors, 44 Bedford Row, London WC1R 4LL. Tel. *071 831 2908*

The Educational Institute of Scotland
The Secretary, 46 Moray Place, Edinburgh, EH3 6BH. Tel. *031-225 6244*

Federation of Associations of College Lecturers in Scotland
The Secretary, 90 Mitchell Street, Glasgow, G1 3NQ. Tel. *041 221 0118*

  Scottish Further and Higher Education Association
The Secretary, 90 Mitchell Street, Glasgow, G1 3NQ. Tel. *041 221 0118*

Headmasters' Conference
The Secretary, 130 Regent Road, Leicester, LE1 7PG. Tel. *0533 854810*

National Association of Head Teachers
The Secretary, 1 Heath Square, Boltro Road, Haywards Heath, West Sussex RH16 1BL. Tel. *0444 458133*

National Association of Inspectors and Educational Advisers
The Secretary, The Old Grammar School, Broadway, Letchworth, Herts SG6 3PP. Tel. *0462 677030*

National Association of Schoolmasters and Union of Women Teachers
The Secretary, Hillscourt Education Centre, Rose Hill, Rednal, Birmingham, B45 8RS. Tel. *021-453 6150.*

National Association of Social Workers in Education
The Secretary, Tanner House, Tanner Street, Thetford, Norfolk. Tel. *3741 or 4484*

National Association of Teachers in Further and Higher Education
The Secretary, 27 Britannia Street, London, WC1X 9JP. Tel. *071-387 3636*

National Society for Education in Art and Design
The Secretary, The Gatehouse, Corsham Court, Corsham, Wiltshire, SN13 0BZ. Tel. *0249 714825*

National Union of Teachers
The Secretary, Hamilton House, Mabledon Place, London, WC1H 9BD. Tel. *071-388 6191*

Northern Ireland Women Teachers' Association
The Secretary, Southlands, 210 Old Ballymena Road, Ballymena BT43 6TS. Tel. *0266 3512*

Professional Association of Nursery Nurses
The Secretary, 99 Friar Gate, Derby DE1 1EZ. Tel. *0332 43029*

Professional Association of Teachers
The Secretary, 99 Friar Gate, Derby, DE1 1EZ. Tel. *372337 STD code 0332*

Scottish Approved Schools Staff Association
The Secretary, Balgowan School, Downfield, Dundee. Tel. *0382 86219*

Scottish Association of Local Government and Education Psychologists
The Secretary, 5 Fairlie Park Drive, Glasgow, G11. Tel. *041 334 4966*

Scottish Secondary Teachers' Association
The Secretary, 15 Dundas Street, Edinburgh. EH3 6QG. Tel. *031-556 5919 and 0605*

Secondary Heads' Association
The Secretary, Chancery House, 107 St. Pauls Road, London N1 2NB. Tel. *071-359 9286*

Undeb Cenedlaethol Athrawon Cymru (National Association of Teachers of Wales)
The Secretary, Prif Swyddfa U.C.A.C. Pen Roc, Rhodfa'r Mor, Aberystwyth, Dyfed. SY23 2AZ. Tel. *0970 615577*

Education (continued)

Ulster Heads Association
The Secretary, Dunluce School, Dunluce Road, Bushmills, Co. Antrim, BT57 8QG. Tel. 026 57 31448.

Ulster Teachers' Union
The Secretary, 94 Malone Road, Belfast, BT9 5HP. Tel. 662216 (STD code 0232)

MEDICAL AND HEALTH SERVICES

Association of British Dental Surgery Assistants
The Secretary, D.S.A. House, 29 London Street, Fleetwood, Lancs. FY7 2JY. Tel. 0253 778631

Association of Clinical Biochemists Ltd.
The Secretary, Burlington House, Piccadilly, London, W1V 0BN. Tel. 071-437 8656

Association of Nurse Administrators
The Secretary, 178 High Holborn, London WC1V 7AN. Tel. 071-240 9784

Association of Optometrists
The Secretary, Bridge House, 233/4 Blackfriars Road, SE1 8NW. Tel. 071-261 9661

Association of Professional Ambulance Personnel
The Secretary, Northfield House, High Street, Castle Cary, Somerset BA7 7AN. Tel. 0963 51188

Association of Professional Music Therapists
The Secretary, 68 Pierce Lane, Fulbourn, Cambridge, CB1 5DL. Tel. 0223 880377

Federation of Professional Organisations
The Secretary, 6–8 Marshalsea Road, London, SE1 1HL. Tel. 071-357 6480

British Dietetic Association
The Secretary, Daimler House, Paradise Street, Birmingham B1 2BJ. Tel. 021-643 5483

British Dental Association
The Secretary, 64 Wimpole Street, London, W1M 8AL. Tel. 071-935 0875

British Hospital Doctors' Federation
The Secretary, The Old Court House, London Road, Ascot, Berkshire SL5 7EN. Tel. 0990 25052

Hospital Consultants' and Specialists' Association
The Secretary, The Old Court House, London Road, Ascot, Berkshire, SL5 7EN. Tel. 0990-25052

Hospital Doctors' Association
The Secretary, The Old Court House, London Road, Ascot, Berks SL5 7EN. Tel. 0990 26613

British Medical Association
The Secretary, British Medical Association House, Tavistock Square, London, WC1H 9JP. Tel. 071-387 4499

British Orthoptic Society
The Secretary, Tavistock House North, Tavistock Square, London WC1H 9HX. Tel. 071 387 7992

Chartered Society of Physiotherapy
The Secretary, 14 Bedford Row, London, WC1R 4ED. Tel. 071-242 1941

Confederation of Health Service Employees
The Secretary, Glen House, High Street, Banstead, Surrey, SM7 2LH. Tel. 0737 353322

District Nursing Association
The Secretary, 31 Castle Terrace, Edinburgh EH1 2EL. Tel. 031-229 2333

English Chiropodists' Association
The Secretary, 42 Velsheda Road, Shirley, Solihull, West Midlands, B90 2JN. Tel. 021-745 1552

Medical and Health Service *(continued)*

General Dental Practitioners' Association
The Secretary, 152 Malden Road, Colchester, CO3 3AY. Tel. *0255 861 829*

Guild of Anatomical Pathology Technicians
The Secretary, 156 Amersham Road, Terrier, High Wycombe. Tel. *071-928 9292
Ext 2926*

Union of Medical Administrative Staff
The Secretary, Adam House, 1 Fitzroy Square, London, W1P 6HE. Tel. *071-387 6046*

Health Visitors' Association
The Secretary, 50 Southwark Street, London, SE1 1UN. Tel. *071-378 7255*

Hospital Physicists' Association
The Secretary, 2 Low Ousegate, York, YO1 1QU. Tel. *0904 610821*

Joint Boots Pharmacists Association
The General Secretary, 7, Dornton Road, South Croydon, Surrey. Tel. *081 688 5688*

Kingswood Pharmacists Association
The Secretary, 18 Croft Close, Braintree, Essex CM7 6EB. Tel. *0376 22337*

Royal College of Midwives
The Secretary, 15 Mansfield Street, London, W1M 0BE. Tel. *071-580 6523*

Royal College of Nursing of the United Kingdom
The Secretary, 20 Cavendish Square, London, W1M 0AB. Tel. *071-409 3333*

Scottish Chiropodists' Association
(Joint Secretaries) 26 Dixon Avenue, Crosshill, Glasgow, G42 8EE. Tel. *041-423 6976*

Scottish Health Visitors' Association
The Secretary, 94 Constitution Street, Leith, Edinburgh EH6 6AW. Tel. *031 553 4061*

Society of Chiropodists
The Secretary, 53 Welbeck Street, London W1M 7HE. Tel. *071-486 3381*

Society of Radiographers
The Secretary, 14 Upper Wimpole Street, London, W1M 8BN. Tel. *071-935 5726*

MISCELLANEOUS SERVICES

Recreational and Cultural Services

Association of Football League Referees and Linesmen
The Secretary, 41 Southdown Drive, Thornton, Cleveleys, Lancs., FY5 5BL. Tel. *0258
860547*

Confederation of Entertainment Unions
The Secretary, 60/62 Clapham Road, London SW9 0JJ. Tel. *071-582 5566*

British Actors' Equity Association
The Secretary, Guild House, Upper St. Martins Lane, London, WC2H 9EG. Tel. *071 379
6000*

Broadcasting, Entertainment and Cinematograph Technicians Union
The Secretary, 111 Wardour St., London W1V 4AY. Tel. *071-437 8506*

Film Artistes' Association
The Secretary, 61 Marloes Road, Kensington, London, W8 6LF. Tel. *071-937 4567*

Musicians' Union
The Secretary, 60–62 Clapham Road, London, SW9 0JJ. Tel. *071-582 5566*

Writers' Guild of Great Britain
The Secretary, 430 Edgware Road, London, W2 1EH. Tel. *071-723 8074*

Cricketers Association
The Secretary, 1A Pargeter Street, Walsall, Staffs.

Recreational and Cultural Services *(continued)*

Federation of Broadcasting Unions
> *The Secretary, Third Floor, King's Court, 2–16 Goodge Street, London, W1P 2AE.* Tel. *071-637 1261*

Federation of Theatre Unions
> *The Secretary, 8 Harley Street, London, W1N 2AB.* Tel. *071-636 6367*

Institute of Football Management and Administration
> *The Secretary, P.O. Box 52, Leamington Spa, Warwicks.* Tel. *0926 882313*

Incorporated Society of Musicians
> *The Secretary, 10 Stratford Place, London, W1N 9AE.* Tel. *071 629 4413*

Guild of Professional Teachers of Dancing
> *The Secretary, 16 Cherry Tree Road, Moreton, Wirral, L46 9RF.* Tel. *051 677 8498*

National Association of Professional and Technical Theatre Personnel
> *The Secretary, 32 Bwllfa Road, Cwmdare, Aberdare, Mid Glamorgan, CF44 8DE.* Tel. *0685 882368*

National Union of Recreation and Sports Employees
> *The Secretary, 39 Mendip Road, Halesowen, West Midlands*

Northern Ireland Musicians' Asociation
> *The Secretary, Crown Chambers, 525 Antrim Road, Belfast, BT15 3BS.* Tel. *370037 (STD code 0232)*

Professional Footballers' Association
> *The Secretary, 2 Oxford Court, Bishopgate, Lower Mosley Street, Manchester, M2 3WQ.* Tel. *061-236 0575*

Stable Lads Association
> *The Secretary, 4 Dunsmore Way Midway, Swadlincote, Derbyshire, DE11 7LA.* Tel. *0283 211522*

The Television and Film Production Employees Association
> *The Secretary, 10 Soho Square, London, W1V 6EE.*

Other Services

Artists Union
> *The Secretary, 9 Poland Street, London, W1V 3DG.* Tel. *071-607 4041*

Association of British Professional Divers
> *The Secretary, 34 Bridge Street, Aberdeen AB1 2JN.* Tel. *0224 590525*

Assistant Chief Probation Officers Association
> *The Secretary, 7 York Avenue, West Kirby, Wirral, Merseyside.*

Association of Staff at Probation and Bail Hostels
> *The Secretary, c/o ILPS, 73 Great Peter Street, London SW1P 2BN.* Tel. *071-222 5656*

Balfour House Staff Association
> *The Secretary, Balfour House, 741 High Road, Finchley, London N12 0BQ.* Tel. *081-446 1477*

British Association of Social Workers
> *The Secretary, Ballylesson Road, Belfast, BT8 8JT*

British Union of Social Work Employees
> *The Secretary, 208 Middleton Road, Manchester M8 6NA.* Tel. *061 720 7727*

Ceram Research Staff Association
> *The Secretary, British Ceramic Research Association, Queens Road, Penkhull, Stoke-on-Trent ST4 7LQ.* Tel. *45431 (STD code 0782)*

Chemistry Societies' Staff Association
> *The Secretary, 31 Hallswelle Road, London NW11 0DH.* Tel. *071-734-9971*

College of Health Care Chaplins
> *Registrar. PO Box 255, Canterbury, Kent, CT2 8AH.* Tel. *0227 455124*

Other Services *(continued)*

Community and Youth Workers Union
> *The Secretary, Unit 202A The Argent Centre, 60 Frederick Street, Birmingham.* Tel.
> *021-233 2815*

Graphic and Creative Arts Association
> *The Secretary, 115 A&B Cleveland Street, London W1P 5PN.* Tel. *071-580 7968*

The Guild of Guide Lecturers
> *The Secretary, 2 Bridge Street, London, SW1A 2JR.* Tel. *071-839 7438*

National Association of Group Secretaries to the National Farmers' Unions
> *The Secretary, Agriculture House, Barker Street, Shrewsbury SY1 1QR.* Tel. *0743 4743*

National Association of Probation Officers
> *The Secretary, 314 Chivalry Road, London SW11 1HT.* Tel. *071 223-4887*

National Association of Senior Probation Officers
> *The Secretary, 37 Bower Mount Road, Maidstone, Kent ME16 8AX.* Tel. *0622 685187*

National League of the Blind and Disabled
> *The Secretary, 2 Tenterden Road, Tottenham, London, N17 8BE.* Tel. *081-808 6030*

Nielson Staff Association
> *The Secretary, Nielson House, Headington, Oxford.* Tel. *0865 742742 Ext. 2291*

Organisation of C.P.L. Technicians
> *The Secretary, Fermor Way, Crowborough, E. Sussex, TN6 3BJ.* Tel. *0892 663842*

Oxfam Staff Association
> *The Secretary, Oxfam House, 274 Banbury Road, Oxford, OX2 7OZ.* Tel. *0865-56777*

Pickfords Travel Staff Association
> *The Secretary, 40 Regent Street, Kingswood, Bristol.*

Potato Marketing Board, Staff Association
> *The Secretary, Hans Crescent, Knightsbridge, London.* Tel. *071-589-4874*

R.S.P.B. Staff Association
> *The Secretary, The Lodge, Sandy, Bedfordshire SG19 2DL.* Tel. *0767 80551*

Society of Authors
> *The Secretary, 84 Drayton Gardens, London SW10 9SB.* Tel. *071-373 6642*

Society of Chief Officers of Probation
> *The Secretary, Gwent Probation Service Headquarters, Cumbrian House, Mamhilad
> Park Estate, Pontypool. NP4 0XD*

Solid Waste Managers' Guild
> *The Secretary, 3 Albion Place, Northampton NN1 1UD.* Tel. *0604 20426*

Sussex Law Clerks' Association
> *The Secretary, c/o Howlett and Clarke, 8 Ship Street, Brighton, BN1 1AZ.* Tel. *0273
> 27272*

NATIONAL ORGANISATIONS COVERING VARIOUS INDUSTRIES

Federation of Industrial Management and Professional Associations
> *The Secretary, 53 St. Michael's Hill, Bristol BS2 8DZ*

Federated Union of Managerial and Professional Officers
> *The Secretary, Terminus House, The High, Harlow, Essex, CM20 1TZ.* Tel. *0279 434444*

Federation of Professional Organisations (P.T. "A" Whitley Council)
> *The Secretary, c/o Society of Radiographers, 14 Upper Wimpole Street, London
> W1M 8BN.* Tel. *071-935 5726*

General Federation of Trade Unions
> *The Secretary, Central House, Upper Woburn Place, London, WC1H 0HY.* Tel. *071-387
> 2578*

National Organisations Covering Various Industries *(continued)*

GMB
> *The Secretary, 22–24 Worple Road, London SW19 4DD.* Tel. *081 947 3131*

Irish Congress of Trade Unions
> *The Secretary, N.I. Officer, Congress House, 3 Wellington Park, Belfast, BT9 6DJ.* Tel. *0232 681726*

Managerial, Professional and Staff Liaison Group (M.P.G.)
> *The Secretary, Tavistock House, Tavistock Square, London WC1H 9JP.* Tel. *071-387 4499 (Switchboard), 01-380 0472 (direct)*

Manufacturing Science Finance Union
> *The Secretary, 79 Camden Road, London NW1 9ES.* Tel. *071-267 4422*

National Institute of Economic and Social Research Staff Association
> *The Secretary, 2 Dean Trench St., London, SW1P 3HE.* Tel. *071-222 7665*

National Union of the Unemployed and Workers
> *The Secretary, 8 Oakwood Road, Lowestoft.* Tel. *0493 514748*

N.U.A.A.W. Organisers' Association
> *The Secretary, 308 Grays Inn Road, London WC1X 8DS.* Tel. *071-278 7801*

Trades Union Congress
> *The Secretary, Congress House, 23–38 Great Russell Street, London, WC1B 3LS.* Tel. *071-636 4030*

Transport and General Workers' Union
> *The Secretary, Transport House, Smith Square, London, SW1P 3JB.* Tel. *071-828 7788*

Scottish Trades Union Congress
> *The Secretary, 12 Woodlands Terrace, Glasgow, G3 6DE.* Tel. *041-332 4946*

Wales Trades Union Council
> *The Secretary, Transport House, 1 Cathedral Road, Cardiff.* Tel. *0222 371495*

Joint Organisations, Wages Councils and Arbitration Boards etc.

Contents

Joint Organisations, Wages Councils and Arbitration Boards, etc.

This list includes all Joint Organisations of Employers and Employees known to the Department to include in their objects the negotiation of wages and/or working conditions and/or the provision of procedures for settling disputes.

The list includes also those joint bodies which make recommendations or report on wages and/or working conditions.

It does not include ad hoc arrangements for negotiation which may be made from time to time between Employers' and Employees' Organisations.

AGRICULTURE FORESTRY AND FISHING

Forestry Commission Industrial and Trade Council
> OFFICIAL SIDE SEC. *Forestry Commission, 231 Corstorphine Road, Edinburgh, EH12 7AT.* Tel. *031-334 0303 Ext. 2300.*
> WORKPEOPLE'S SEC. *Transport & General Workers Union, Transport House, Smith Square, London, SW1P 3JB*, Tel. *01-828 7788*

ENERGY AND WATER SUPPLY

Coal Mining

National Arbitration Panel (Between British Coal Corporation and the Union of Democratic Mineworkers, for mineworkers and daily paid industrials at National Workshops)
> EMPLOYERS SIDE. *British Coal Corporation, Eastwood Hall, Eastwood, Nottingham, NG16 3EB.* Tel. *0773 531313*
> EMPLOYEES SIDE. *U.D.M., The Sycamores, Bestwood, Nottingham, NG6 8UE.* Tel. *0602 763468*

National Conciliation Committee
All details as above

National Conciliation Council for the Coal Mining Industry, Officials (Overmen and Deputies) National Joint Council
> EMPLOYERS SIDE. *British Coal Corporation, Eastwood Hall, Eastwood, Nottingham, NG16 3EB.* Tel. *0773 531313.*
> EMPLOYEES SIDE. *NACODS, Simpson House, 48 Netherall Road, Doncaster, Sth Yorkshire DN1 2PZ.* Tel. *0302 68015*

Conciliation Agreement for Management and Junior Technical Staff in the Coal Mining Industry National Joint Council
> EMPLOYERS SIDE. *British Coal Corporation, Hobart House, 36–42 Grosvenor Place, London, SW1X 7AE.* Tel. *071-235 2020.*
> EMPLOYEES SEC. *B.A.C.M. House, 317 Nottingham Road, Old Basford, Nottingham, NG7 7DP.* Tel. *0602 785819*

Conciliation Agreement for Clerical and Junior Administrative Staff in the Coal Mining Industry National Joint Council
> EMPLOYEES SIDE. *British Coal Corporation, Hobart House 36–42 Grosvenor Place, London, SW1X 7AE.* Tel. *071-235 2020.*
> EMPLOYEES SIDE. *Apex Partnership. 22–24 Worple Road London, SW19 4DD.* Tel. *081 947 3131.*

National Reference Tribunals
(1) British Association of Colliery Management Conciliation Scheme
(2) Officials Conciliation Scheme
(3) Clerical and Junior Administrative Staff Conciliation Scheme
The Secretary, Fountain Court, Temple, London EC4 9DH. Tel. *071-583 3335*

Manufacture of Solid Fuels

National Conciliation Board for the Coal Mining Industry, Coke and By-products Group National Joint Council
> *The Secretary, British Coal, Hobart House. 36–42 Grosvenor Place, London, SW1X 7AE. Tel. 071-235 2020. P. Heathfield, National Union of Mineworkers, St James's House, Vicar Lane, Sheffield, South Yorkshire, S1 2EX. Tel. 0742 700388.*

Manufacture of Solid Fuels *(continued)*

National Conciliation Board for the Coal Mining Industry, Coke and By-products group
  National Reference Tribunal
      The Secretary, Fountain Court, Temple, London EC4 9DH. Tel. *071-353 7356*

Gas

British Gas National Joint Council for Higher Management
      EMPLOYERS SEC. *British Gas plc, Rivermill House, 152 Grosvenor Road, London,
      SW1V 3JL.* Tel. *071-821 1444*
      EMPLOYEE'S SIDE. *Epic House (5.2A), Charles Street, Leicester, LE1 3SH.* Tel. *0533
      539071.*

British Gas National Joint Council for Gas Staffs and Senior Officers
      EMPLOYERS' SEC. *British Gas plc, Rivermill House, 152 Grosvenor Road, London, SW1V
      3JL.* Tel. *071-821 1444*
      WORKPEOPLE'S SEC. *National and Local Government Officers' Association, Nalgo House, 1
      Mabledon Place, London, WC1H 9AJ.* Tel. *071-388 2366*

British Gas National Joint Industrial Council
      EMPLOYERS' SEC. *British Gas plc, 152 Grosvenor Road, London, SW1V 3JL.* Tel. *071-821
      1444*
      WORKPEOPLE'S SEC. *GMB, 22–24 Worple Road, London SW19 4DD.* Tel. *081 947 3131*

Electricity

National Joint Council (Professional Administrative, Clerical & Sales Staff) for the Electricity
  Supply Industry
      EMPLOYERS' SEC. *The Electricity Council, 30 Millbank, London, SW1P 4RD.* Tel. *071-834
      2333*
      WORKPEOPLE'S SEC. *National and Local Government Officers Association, 1 Mabledon
      Place, London, WC1H 9AJ.* Tel. *071-388 2366*

National Joint Board (Technical Engineering Staff) (Electricity Supply Industry)
      EMPLOYERS' SEC. *The Electricity Council, 30 Millbank, London, SW1P 4RD.* Tel. *071-834
      2333*
      WORKPEOPLE'S SEC. *Electrical Power Engineers' Association, 6th Floor, James House,
      Welford, Leicester, LE2 7A.* Tel. *053 548266*

National Joint (Building and Civil Engineering) Committee (Electricity Supply Industry)
      EMPLOYERS' SEC. *The Electricity Council, 30 Millbank, London, SW1P 4RD.* Tel. *071-834
      2333*
      OPERATIVES' SEC. *U.C.A.T.T. House, 177 Abbeville Road, Clapham, London, SW4 9RL.* Tel.
      071-622 2442

National Joint Industrial Council (Electricity Supply Industry)
      EMPLOYERS' SEC. *The Electricity Council, 30 Millbank, London, SW1P 4RD.* Tel. *071-834
      2333*
      WORKPEOPLE'S SEC. *GMB, 22–24 Worple Road, London SW19 4DD.* Tel. *081 947 3131*

National Joint Managerial and Higher Executive Grades Committee for the Electricity Supply
  Industry
      EMPLOYERS' SEC. *The Electricity Council, 30 Millbank, London SW1P 4RD.* Tel. *071-834
      2333*
      WORKPEOPLE'S SEC. *E.P.E.A., Station House, Fox Lane, Chertsey, Surrey, KT16 9HW.* Tel.
      0932 564131

Northern Ireland Electricity Supply Industry Joint Board
      EMPLOYERS' SEC. *N.I.E.S., 120 Malone Road, Belfast, BT9 5HT.* Tel. *661100.*
      WORKPEOPLE'S SEC. *E.P.E.A., Station House, Fox Lane North, Chertsey, Surrey, KT16
      9HW.* Tel. *0932 564131*

Northern Ireland Electricity Supply Industry Joint Industrial Council
      EMPLOYERS' SEC. *N.I.E.S., Danesfort, 120 Malone Road, Belfast, BT9 5HT.* Tel. *661100
      Ext. 2213*
      WORKPEOPLE'S SEC. *E.E.T.P.U., A. E. U. House, 1A Adela Street, Belfast, BT14 6AW.* Tel.
      740244/5/6.

Northern Ireland Electricity Supply Industry Joint Managerial and Higher Executive Grades
  Committee
      EMPLOYERS' SEC. *N.I.E.S., P.O. Box 2, 120 Malone Road, Belfast, BT9 5HT.* Tel. *0232
      661100*

Electricity *(continued)*

EMPLOYEES' SEC. *E.P.E.A., Station House, Fox Lane North, Chertsey, Surrey, KT16 9HW.* Tel. *0932 564131*

Northern Ireland Electricity Joint Council (Administrative and Clerical Grades)
EMPLOYERS' SEC. *N.I.E.S., 120 Malone Road, Belfast, BT9 5HT.* Tel. *661100*
EMPLOYEES' SEC. *A.P.E.X., 291 Antrim Road, Belfast, BT15 2GZ.* Tel. *748678 (STD code 0232)*

Nuclear

National Joint Industrial Council for the United Kingdom Atomic Energy Authority
EMPLOYERS' SEC. *Employee Relations Branch, United Kingdom Atomic Energy Authority, 11 Charles II Street, London, SW1Y 4QP.* Tel. *01-930 5454 Ext. 542*
WORKPEOPLE'S SEC. *T.G.W.U., Transport House, Smith Square, London, SW1P 3JB.* Tel. *071-828 7788*

Whitley Council for the United Kingdom Atomic Energy Authority
EMPLOYERS' SEC. *Employee Relations Branch, United Kingdom Atomic Energy Authority, 11 Charles II Street, London, SW1Y 4QP.* Tel. *071-930 5454 Ext. 542*
WORKPEOPLE'S SEC. *United Kingdom Atomic Energy Authority, 11 Charles II Street, London, SW1Y 4QP.* Tel. *071-930 5454 Ext. 417*

EXTRACTION OF MINERALS AND ORES OTHER THAN FUELS

Stone, Clay, Sand and Gravel

China Clay Production Joint Negotiating Committee
EMPLOYERS' SEC. *E.C.C. International Ltd., John Keay House, St. Austell, Cornwall, PL25 4DJ.* Tel. *St. Austell (0726) 623422*
WORKPEOPLE'S SEC. *Transport and General Workers' Union, 1A High Cross Street, St. Austell, Cornwall, PL25 4AB.* Tel. *75110-73694 (STD code 0726)*

National Joint Industrial Council for the Roadstone Quarrying Industry
EMPLOYERS' SEC. *F.C.A., c/o Arthur Young C.A., Norham House, Fourth Floor, 12 New Bridge Street, Newcastle upon Tyne, NE1 8AD.* Tel. *2611063 (STD code 091)*
WORKPEOPLE'S SEC. *T.G.W.U. Transport House, Smith Square, London, SW1P 3JB.* Tel. *071-828 7788*

Northern Ireland Joint Industrial Council for the Quarrying Industry
EMPLOYERS' SEC. *Jackson Andrews, Chartered Accountants, Andras House, 60 Great Victoria Street, Belfast, BT2 7ET.* Tel. *233152 (STD code 0232)*
WORKPEOPLE'S SEC. *Amalgamated Transport and General Workers Union, 102 High Street, Belfast, BT1 2BG.* Tel. *0232 232381*

METAL MANUFACTURE

Galvanising Conciliation Board
EMPLOYERS' SEC. *British Steel plc, P.O. Box 10, Newport Gwent, NP9 0XN.* Tel. *0633 290022 Ext. 4171*
WORKPEOPLE'S SEC. *T.G.W.U., Transport House, Smith Square, London, SW1P 3TB.* Tel. *071-828 7788*

Joint Industrial Council for the Wire and Wire Rope Industries
EMPLOYERS' SEC. *Wire and Wire Rope Employers Association, 6 Brome Way, Spital, Wirral, Merseyside, L63 9ND.* Tel. *051 346 1566*
EMPLOYEES' SEC. *Wire Workers Union, Prospect House, Alma Street, Sheffield, South Yorkshire, S3 8SA.* Tel. *Sheffield (0742) 21674*

Sheet Trade Board
EMPLOYERS' SEC. *British Steel plc, P.O. Box 10, Newport, Gwent, NP9 0XN.* Tel. *0633 290022 Ext. 4171.*
WORKPEOPLE'S SEC. *Iron and Steel Trades Confederation, Swinton House, 324 Gray's Inn Road, London, WC1X 8DD.* Tel. *071-837 6691*

Metal Manufacture *(continued)*

Welsh Engineers' and Founders' Conciliation Board
>   EMPLOYERS' SEC. *Welsh Engineers' and Founders' Association, 11 St. James' Gardens, Swansea, SA1 6DY.* Tel. *0792 472837*
>   WORKPEOPLE'S SEC. *West Wales Allied Engineering Trades Committee, A.U.E.W. House, 34 Orchard Street, Swansea, SA1 5AW.* Tel. *0792-54398*

MANUFACTURE OF NON-METALLIC MINERAL PRODUCTS

Bricks, Fireclay and Refractory Goods

Joint Negotiating Committee for the Fletton Brick Industry
>   EMPLOYER'S SEC. *London Brick Co. Ltd., P.O. Box 259, Marston Road, Marston Morteyne, Bedford, MK43 0YJ.* Tel. *0525 405858 Ext. 219*
>   EMPLOYEE'S SEC. *A.E.U. House, 396–398 Dunstable Road, Luton, Bedford, LU4 8JT.* Tel. *(0582) 576271*

National Joint Council for the Building Brick and Allied Industries
>   EMPLOYERS' SEC. *National Federation of Clay Industries, Federation House, Station Road, Stoke on Trent, ST4 2SA.* Tel. *0782 747256*
>   WORKPEOPLE'S SEC. *GMB, 22–24 Worple Road, London SW19 4DD.* Tel. *081 947 3131*

National Joint Wages Board for the Refractories Industry
>   EMPLOYER'S SEC. *National Federation of Clay Industries, Federation House, Station Road, Stoke on Trent, ST4 2SA.* Tel. *0782 747256*
>   WORKPEOPLE'S SEC. *GMB, 22–24 Worple Road, London SW19 4DD.* Tel. *081 947 3131*

Glass and Ceramic Goods

National Joint Council for the Ceramic Industry
>   EMPLOYERS' SEC. *British Ceramic Manufacturers Federation, Federation House, Station Road, Stoke-on-Trent, ST4 2SA.* Tel. *0782 744631*
>   EMPLOYEES' SEC. *Ceramic and Allied Trades Union, 5 Hillcrest House, Garth Street, Hanley, Stoke-on-Trent, ST2 3AB.* Tel. *0782 272755*

National Joint Council for the Flat Glass Industry
>   EMPLOYERS' SEC. *Flat Glass Council, c/o Glass and Glazing Federation, 44–48 Borough High Street, London, SE1 1XB.* Tel. *071-403 7177*
>   WORKPEOPLE'S JOINT SECS. *E.E.T.P.U., Hayes Court, West Common Road, Hayes, Bromley, BR2 7AU.* Tel. *081-462 7755. FTAT, "Fairfields", Roe Green, Kingsbury, London, NW9 0PT.* Tel. *081-204 0273. F. G. Smith, Sogat 82 (Sign and Display), 274–288 London Road, Hadleigh, Benfleet, Essex, S57 2DE.* Tel. *0702 554111*

Miscellaneous Building Materials

Joint Industrial Council for the Pre-Cast Concrete Industry in Scotland
>   EMPLOYERS' SEC. *9 Princes Street, Falkirk, FK1 1LS.* Tel. *22088 (STD code 0324)*
>   WORKPEOPLE'S SEC. *Transport and General Workers' Union, 46 Main Street, Wishaw, ML2 7AJ.* Tel. *069-83-74875*

National Joint Council for the Monumental Masonry Industry
>   EMPLOYERS' SEC. *National Association of Master Masons, Crown Buildings, High Street, Aylesbury, Bucks, HP20 15L.* Tel. *(0296) 434750*
>   WORKPEOPLE'S SEC. *Union of Construction, Allied Trades and Technicians, U.C.A.T.T. House, 177 Abbeville Road, Clapham, London, SW4 9RL.* Tel. *071-622 2442*

National Joint Industrial Council for the Cast Stone and Cast Concrete Products Industry
>   EMPLOYERS' SEC. *F.C.I.S., The British Precast Concrete Federation Ltd., 60 Charles Street, Leicester, LE1 1FB.* Tel. *0533 536161*
>   WORKPEOPLE'S SEC. *Transport and General Workers' Union, Transport House, Smith Square, London, SW1P 3JB.* Tel. *071-828 7788*

National Joint Council for the Ready Mixed Concrete Industry
>   EMPLOYERS' SEC. *British Ready Mixed Concrete Association, 1 Bramber Court, 2 Bramber Road, London, W14 9PB.* Tel. *071-381 6582*
>   WORKPEOPLES' SEC. *Transport and General Workers' Union, Transport House, Smith Square, London, SW1P 3JB.* Tel. *071-828 7788*

Miscellaneous Building Materials *(continued)*

National Joint Industrial Council for the Slag Industry
>EMPLOYERS' SEC. *Tarmac Roadstone Ltd., John Hadfield House, Dale Rd., Matlock, Derbyshire.* Tel. *(0629) 3456 Ext. 441*
>WORKPEOPLE'S SEC. *Iron and Steel Trades Confederation, Swinton House, 342 Gray's Inn Road, London, WC1X 8DD.* Tel. *071-837 6691*

CHEMICAL INDUSTRY

Chemical and Allied Industries Joint Industrial Council
>EMPLOYERS' SEC. *Industrial Relations Director, Chemical Industries Association Limited, Kings Buildings, Smith Square, London, SW1P 3JJ.* Tel. *071-834 3399*
>WORKPEOPLE'S SEC. *T.G.W.U., Transport House, Smith Square, London, SW1P 3JB.* Tel. *071-828 7788*

Pharmaceuticals and Fine Chemicals Joint Industrial Council
>EMPLOYERS' SEC. *Deputy Director, Employee Relations, Chemical Industries Association Limited, Kings Buildings, Smith Square, London, SW1P 3JJ.* Tel. *071-834 3399*
>WORKPEOPLE'S SEC. *Union of Shop, Distributive and Allied Workers, 188 Wilmslow Road, Fallowfield, Manchester, M14 6LJ.* Tel. *061-224 2804*

METAL GOODS, ENGINEERING AND VEHICLES

Vehicles, Aircraft and Aerospace

Railway Shopmen's National Council
>EMPLOYERS' SEC. *Room 320, British Railways Board Headquarters, Rail House, Euston Square, London, NW1 2DZ.* Tel. *262-3232 Ext. 7675*
>JOINT WORKPEOPLE'S SECS. *Unity House, 203 Euston Road, London, NW1 2BL.* Tel. *91-387 4711. 140–142 Walworth Road, London SE17 1JW.* Tel. *071-703 2215*

Railway Workshop Supervisory Staff National Council
>EMPLOYERS' SEC. *Room 312, British Railways Board Headquarters, Rail House, Euston Square, London, NW1 2DZ.* Tel. *071-262 3232 Ext. 7669*
>WORKPEOPLE'S SEC. *Secretary, Railway Workshop Supervisory Committee, Unity House, 203 Euston Road, London, NW1 2BL.* Tel. *071-387 4771*

Miscellaneous Engineering Production

Joint Board of the British Cutlery and Silverware Association and the M.S.F.
>EMPLOYERS' SEC. *Light Trades House, 3 Melbourne Avenue, Sheffield, S10 2QJ.* Tel. *663084 (STD code 0742)*
>WORKPEOPLE'S SEC. *M.S.F., 61 Wolstenholme Road, Sheffield, S7 1LE.* Tel. *0742 589433*

Joint Industrial Council for the Cable Employers' Association
>EMPLOYERS' SEC. *Cable Employers' Association, 56 Palace Road, East Molesey, Surrey, KT8 9DW.* Tel. *081-941 4079*
>WORKPEOPLE'S SEC. *T.G.W.U., Transport House, Smith Square, London, SW1P 3JB.* Tel. *071-828 7788*

Joint Industrial Council for the Lock, Latch and Key Industry
>JOINT SEC. *E. C. Skelding Associates, The Office, Heath Street, Tamworth, Staffs, B79 7JH.* Tel. *0827 52337*

National Association of Farriers, Blacksmiths and Agricultural Engineers
>JOINT SEC. *Avenue R, 7th Street, R.A.C. Stoneleigh, Warwicks, CV8 2LG.* Tel. *0203 696595*

National Joint Council for the Craft of Dental Technicians
>EMPLOYERS' SEC. *British Dental Association, 64 Wimpole Street, London, W1M 8AL.* Tel. *071-935 0875*
>WORKPEOPLE'S SEC. *Union of Shop, Distributive and Allied Workers, "Oakley", 188 Wilmslow Road, Manchester, M14 6LJ.* Tel. *061-224 2804*

National Joint Council for the Stamped or Pressed Metal Wares Industry
>EMPLOYERS' SEC. *E. C. Skelding Associates, The Office, Heath Street, Tamworth, Staffs, B79 7JH.* Tel. *0827 52337*

Miscellaneous Engineering Production (*continued*)

WORKPEOPLE'S SEC. *GMB 22–24 Worple Road, London SW19 4DD* Tel. *081 947 3131.*

FOOD DRINK AND TOBACCO

Bacon and Meat Products

Bacon Curing Industry National Joint Industrial Council
EMPLOYERS' SEC. *19 Cornwall Terrace, London, NW1 4QP.* Tel. *071-935 7980*
WORKPEOPLES' SEC. *Transport and General Workers' Union, Transport House, Smith Square, London, SW1P 3JB.* Tel. *071-828 7788*

Joint Industrial Council for the Food Manufacturers' Industrial Group
EMPLOYERS' SEC. *6 Catherine Street, London WC2B 5JJ.* Tel. *071-836 2460*
WORKPEOPLE'S SEC. *Transport House, Smith Square, London, SW1P 3JB.* Tel. *071-828 7788*

Milk Products

Joint Industrial Council for the Milk Processing Industry in Northern Ireland
EMPLOYERS' SEC. *Northern Dairies (Ireland) Limited, 123/137 York Street, Belfast, BT15 1AB.* Tel. *0232 248385*
WORKPEOPLE'S SEC. *A.T.G.W.U., 27 New Row, Coleraine, Co. Londonderry, BT52 1AD.* Tel. *Coleraine 3386 (0265)*

National Joint Council for the Dairy Industry in England and Wales
EMPLOYERS' SEC. *The Dairy Trade Federation Ltd, 19 Cornwall Terrace, London, NW1 4QP.* Tel. *071-486-7244*
EMPLOYEES' SEC. *T.G.W.U., Transport House, Smith Square, London, SW1P 3JB.* Tel. *071-828-7788*

Miscellaneous Food and Drink

Joint Industrial Council for the Biscuit Industry
EMPLOYERS' SEC. *Biscuit, Cake Chocolate and Confectionery Alliance, 11 Green Street, London, W1Y 3RF.* Tel. *071 629 8971.*
WORKPEOPLE'S SEC. *GMB 22–24 Worple Road, London SW19 4DD.* Tel. *081 947 3131*

National Joint Industrial Council for the Seed Crushing, Compound and Provender Manufacturing Industries
EMPLOYERS' SEC. *c/o BOCM Silcock Limited, Basing View, Basingstoke, Hampshire, RG21 2EQ.* Tel. *0256-843210*
WORKPEOPLE'S SEC. *Transport and General Workers' Union, Transport House, Smith Square, London, SW1P 3JB.* Tel. *071-828 7788*

National Joint Trades Union Negotiating Committee
EMPLOYERS' REPRESENTATIVE. *British Sugar Corporation plc, P.O. Box 26, Oundle Road, Peterborough, PE2 9QU.* Tel. *0733 63171*
WORKPEOPLE'S SEC. *Transport and General Workers' Union, 34 Coweate, Peterborough, PE1 1NA.* Tel. *0733 62152*
EMPLOYEES' SEC. *A.T.G.W.U., 20 High Street, Omagh, Co. Tyrone, BT78 1BQ.* Tel. *0662 3326*

Scottish Bakery Joint Industrial Council
EMPLOYERS' SEC. *Scottish Association of Master Bakers, Atholl House, 4 Torphichen St., Edinburgh, EH3 8JQ.* Tel. *031-229 1401*
WORKPEOPLE'S SEC. *Union of Shop, Distributive and Allied Workers, 188 Wilmslow Road, Manchester, M14 6LJ.* Tel. *061-224 2804*

Tobacco

National Joint Council for the Tobacco Industry
JOINT SEC. *Tobacco Industry Employers' Association, Glen House, Stag Place, London, SW1E 5AG.* Tel. *071-828 2041*

TEXTILES

Woollen and Worsted

The West of England Joint Industrial Council for the Woollen and Worsted Trades
EMPLOYERS' SEC. *Lodgemore Mills, Stroud, Gloucestershire.* Tel. *045-36 3373*

Woollen and Worsted (continued)

EMPLOYEES' SEC. *T.G.W.U., 18 Worcester Street, Gloucester, GL1 3AE. Tel. 0452 423701*

Hosiery and Knitted Goods

Joint Negotiating Committee for the Scottish Knitwear Trade
EMPLOYERS' SEC. *55 John Finnie Street, Kilmarnock, KA1 1HQ. Tel. 0563-23568*
WORKPEOPLE'S SEC. *National Union of Hosiery and Knitwear Workers, 6 Portland Road, Kilmarnock, KA1 2BS. Tel. 0563 27476*

National Joint Industrial Council for the Hosiery and Knitwear Industry
EMPLOYERS' SEC. *The Knitting Industries' Federation Ltd., 7 Gregory Boulevard, Nottingham, NG7 6NB. Tel. (0602) 621081*
WORKPEOPLE'S SEC. *Nat. Union of Hosiery and Knitwear Workers, 55 New Walk, Leicester, LE1 7EB. Tel. 556703 (STD code 0533)*

Carpets

National Joint Committee for the Carpet Industry
EMPLOYERS' SEC. *British Carpet Manufacturers' Association Limited, 72 Dean Street, London, W1V 5HB. Tel. 071-734 9853*
WORKPEOPLE'S SEC. *National Affiliation of Carpet Trade Unions, Carpet Weavers' Hall, Callows Lane, Kidderminster, Worcestershire, DY10 2JG. Tel. 823192 (STD code 0562)*

Narrow Fabrics

Joint Industrial Council for the Narrow Fabrics Industry
EMPLOYERS' SEC.. *4th Floor, York House, 91 Granby Street, Leicester, LE1 6EA. Tel. (0533) 545490.*
WORKPEOPLE'S SEC. *GMB, 22–24 Worple Road, London SW19 4DD. Tel. 081 947 3131.*

General Textiles and Trades

Jute and Allied Textiles Joint Council (Dundee Area)
EMPLOYERS' SIDE. *East of Scotland Textiles Employers' Industrial Association, 148 Nethergate, Dundee, DD1 4EA. Tel. 0382 25881*
EMPLOYEES' SIDE. *T.G.W.U., 32/34 Dock Street, Dundee, Scotland, DD1 3DR.*

National Joint Industrial Council for the Surgical Dressings Industry
EMPLOYERS' SEC. *Hinders Leslies Ltd, Green Pond Road, London, EI7 6EN.*
WORKPEOPLE'S SEC. *GMB, 22–24 Worple Road, London SW19 4DD. Tel. 081 947 3131*

Textile Finishing Trade Conciliation Board
EMPLOYERS' SEC. *British Textile Employers' Association, Reedham House, 31 King Street West, Manchester, M3 2PF. Tel. 061-834 7871*
WORKPEOPLE'S SEC. *T.G.W.U., Textile Trade Group, National House, Sunbridge Road, Bradford, BD1 2QB. Tel. 0274-725642*

LEATHER AND LEATHER GOODS

British Leathergoods Manufacturers Association
EMPLOYERS' SEC. *27 Frederick Street, Birmingham, B1 3HJ. Tel. 021-236-2657*
WORKPEOPLE'S SEC. *Madeup Leathergood Section, National Union of Footwear, Leather and Allied Trades, Leather Trade Group, The Grange, Earls Barton, Northampton, NN6 0JH. Tel. 810326*

FOOTWEAR AND CLOTHING

Footwear

The Board of Conciliation and Arbitration for the Boot and Shoe Trade of London
JOINT SEC. *84–88 Great Eastern Street, London EC2A 3PX. Tel. 071-739 1678*

Board of Conciliation and Arbitration for the Boot and Shoe Trade of Northern Ireland
JOINT SEC. *Down Shoes, 37 Edenvale Avenue, Banbridge, Co. Down, BT32 3RH. Tel. Banbridge 23909*

Footwear *(continued)*

Boot and Shoe Manufacturing Trade National Joint Standing Committee
EMPLOYERS' SEC. *British Footwear Manufacturers' Federation, Royalty House, 72 Dean Street, London, W1V 5HB.* Tel. *071-437 5573*
WORKPEOPLE'S SEC. *National Union of Footwear, Leather and Allied Trades, The Grange, Earls Barton, Northampton, NN6 0JH.* Tel. *Northampton 810326 (STD code 0604)*

Kingswood and District Conciliation and Arbitration Board for the Boot and Shoe Trade
HON. SEC. *c/o G. B. Britton, Lodge Road, Kingswood, Bristol, BS15 1JB.* Tel. *0272-352777*
EMPLOYEES' SEC. *National Union of Footwear Leather and Allied Trades, 15–17 High Street, Kingswood, Bristol.* Tel. *0273 673116*

Leeds Board of Conciliation and Arbitration for the Boot and Shoe Trade
JOINT SEC. *Gola Lamb Ltd., Bottomboat Road, Stanley, Wakefield, W. Yorkshire, WF3 4AY.* Tel. *0924 823541.*

Leicester Board of Conciliation and Arbitration for the Boot and Shoe Trade
JOINT SEC. *Leicester and County F.M.A., 4th Floor, York House, 91 Granby Street, Leicester, LE1 6FB.* Tel. *0533-556646*

Leicestershire and Rutland Board of Conciliation and Arbitration for the Boot and Shoe Trade
JOINT SEC. *Leicester and County F.M.A., 4th Floor, York House, 91 Granby Street, Leicester, LE1 6FB.* Tel. *0533-556646*

Norwich and District Board of Conciliation and Arbitration for the Boot and Shoe Trade
EMPLOYERS' SEC. *c/o Bally Shoe Factories Ltd., Hall Road, Norwich, NR4 6DP.* Tel. *761100 (STD code 0603)*
WORKPEOPLE'S SEC. *N.U.F.L.A.T., 5 Taverners Square, Silver Road, Norwich.* Tel. *(0603) 629027*

Stafford and District Board of Conciliation and Arbitration for the Boot and Shoe Industry
JOINT SEC. *Lotus Ltd., Freemen Street, Stafford, ST16 3JA.* Tel. *223200 (STD code 0785)*
EMPLOYEES' SEC. *National Union of Footwear, Leather and Allied Trades, Sheridan Hall, Sandon Road, Stafford, ST16 3HF.* Tel. *0785-58379*

Clothing, Hats and Gloves

London Joint Conciliation Board
EMPLOYERS' SEC. *Federation of Merchant Tailors, 32 Savile Row, London W1X 1AG.* Tel. *071-734-0171*
WORKPEOPLES' SEC. *GMB, 22–24 Worple Road, London SW19 4DD.* Tel. *081 947 3131*

TIMBER AND FURNITURE

Bedding and Mattress Manufacturing Trade Joint Industrial Council
EMPLOYERS' SEC. *National Bedding Federation, 251 Brompton Road, London, SW3 2EZ.* Tel. *071-589 4888*
WORKPEOPLE'S SEC. *Furniture, Timber and Allied Trades Union, "Fairfields", Roe Green, Kingsbury, London, NW9 0PT.* Tel. *081-204 0273*

British Furniture Trade Joint Industrial Council
EMPLOYERS' SEC. *British Furniture Manufacturers Federation, 30 Harcourt Street, London, W1H 2AA.* Tel. *071-724 0854*
WORKERS SIDE SEC. *F.T.A.T.U., "Fairfields", Roe Green, Kingsbury, London, NW9 0PT.* Tel. *081-204 0273*

Joint Council for the Furniture Industry (Northern Ireland)
EMPLOYERS' SEC. *13 Carolsteen Avenue, Helens Bay, Co. Down, BT19 1LJ.* Tel. *0247 852869*
WORKPEOPLE'S SEC. *52 Peter's Hill, Belfast, BT13 2AB.* Tel. *0232 243588*

Timber and Furniture *(continued)*

National Conciliation Board for the Upholstery, Bedding and Other Fillings Materials
　　Manufacturing Trades
　　　EMPLOYERS' SEC. *National Fillings Trades Association, 23 Raleigh Street, Islington,*
　　　　London, N1 8NP. Tel. *071-226 3407*
　　　WORKPEOPLE'S SEC. *"Fairfields", Roe Green, Kingsbury, London, NW9 0PT*. Tel. *081-204*
　　　　0273

National Joint Council for Building and Allied Hardware Manufacturers Federation
　　　EMPLOYERS' SEC. *5 Greenfield Crescent, Edgbaston, Birmingham, B15 3BE*. Tel. *021-454*
　　　　2177
　　　WORKPEOPLE'S SEC. *National Society of Metal Mechanics, 70 Lionel Street, Birmingham,*
　　　　B3 1JG. Tel. *021-236 1726*

National Joint Council for the Exhibition Industry
　　　EMPLOYERS' SEC. *British Exhibition Contractors Association, Kingsmere House, Graham*
　　　　Road, Wimbledon, London, SW19 3SR. Tel. *081-543 3888*
　　　WORKPEOPLE'S SEC. *U.C.A.T.T. House, 177 Abbeville Road,* London, SW4 9RL. Tel. *071*
　　　　622 2442

National Joint Industrial Council for the British Veneer Producing and Plywood Manufacturing
　　Industry
　　　EMPLOYERS' SEC. *Spectrum House, 20–26 Cursitor Street, London EC4A 1HY* . Tel. *071*
　　　　405 2088
　　　WORKPEOPLE'S SEC. *GMB, 22–24 Worple Road, London SW19 4DD*. Tel. *081 947 3131*

National Joint Industrial Council for the Home Grown Timber Trade
　　　EMPLOYERS' SEC. *B.T.M.A. (England and Wales), Ridgeway House, 6 Ridgeway Road,*
　　　　Long Ashton, Bristol, BS18 9EU. Tel. *0272 394022*
　　　WORKPEOPLE'S SEC. *Transport and General Workers Union, Transport House, Smith*
　　　　Square, London, SW1P 3JB. Tel. *071-828 7788*

MISCELLANEOUS MANUFACTURING INDUSTRIES

Joint Industrial Council of the Match Manufacturing Industry
　　　SEC. *Bryant & May Ltd., Mersey Works, Speke Road, Liverpool, L19 2PH*. Tel. *051 494*
　　　　9555
　　　WORKPEOPLE'S SEC. *Bryant and May Ltd., Mersey Works, Speke Road, Liverpool, L19*
　　　　2PH. Tel. *051-494 9555*

Joint Industrial Council for the Pianoforte Manufacturing Trade
　　　EMPLOYERS' SEC. *Pianoforte Manufacturers and Distributors Association Ltd., 22 Beach*
　　　　Road, Lowestoft, Suffolk, NR32 1EA. Tel. *0502 69931*
　　　WORKPEOPLE'S SEC. *F.T.A.T.U., "Fairfields", Roe Green, Kingsbury, London, NW9 0PT*.
　　　　Tel. *081-204 0273*

CONSTRUCTION

Building and Allied Trades Joint Industrial Council
　　　EMPLOYERS' SEC. *Federation of Master Builders, Gordon Fisher House, 33 John Street,*
　　　　London WC2N 2BB. Tel. *071-242 7583*
　　　OPERATIVES SEC. *T.G.W.U., Transport House, Smith Square, London, SW1P 3JB*. Tel.
　　　　071-828 7788

Civil Engineering Construction Conciliation Board for Great Britain
　　　EMPLOYERS' SEC. *Cowdray House, 6 Portugal Street, London, WC2A 3HH*. Tel. *071-404*
　　　　4020
　　　OPERATIVES SEC. *T.G.W.U., Transport House, Smith Square, London, SW1P 3JB*. Tel.
　　　　071-828 7788

Demolition Industry Conciliation Board
　　　EMPLOYERS' SEC. *National Federation of Demolition Contractors, Cowdray House, 6*
　　　　Portugal Street, London, WC2A 2HH. Tel. *071-404 4020*
　　　OPERATIVES' SEC. *T.G.W.U., Transport House, Smith Square, London, SW1P 3JB*. Tel.
　　　　071-828 7788

Construction *(continued)*

Isle of Man Joint Industrial Council (Building Industry)
> EMPLOYERS' SEC. *Employers Federation, Herondean, Trossach Road, Ballasalla, Isle of Man*. Tel. *0624-824454*
> EMPLOYEES' SEC. *39 Bermahague Avenue, Onchan, Isle of Man*. Tel. *0624 27863*.

Joint Council for the Building and Civil Engineering Industry (Northern Ireland)
> EMPLOYERS' SEC. *The Federation of Building & Civil Engineering Contractors (N.I.) Ltd., 143 Malone Road, Belfast, BT9 6SX*. Tel. *0232-661711*
> WORKPEOPLE'S SEC. *Union of Construction, Allied Trades and Technicians, 79–81 May Street, Belfast, BT1 3JL*. Tel. *322366 (STD code 0232)*

Joint Industry Board for the Electrical Contracting Industry
> JOINT SEC. *Kingswood House, 47–51 Sidcup Hill, Sidcup, Kent, DA14 6HP*. Tel. *081-302 0031*

Joint Industry Board for Plumbing Mechanical Engineering Services in England and Wales
> JOINT SEC. *(Director), Brook House, Brook Street, St. Neots, Huntingdon, Cambridgeshire, PE19 2HW*. Tel. *76925 (STD code 0480)*

National Joint Committee for the Plastering Craft in Scotland
> EMPLOYERS' SEC. *Scottish Master Plasterers Association, 12 Hill Street, Edinburgh, EH2 3LB*. Tel. *031-225 5214*
> WORKPEOPLE'S SEC. *T.G.W.U., 290 Bath Street, Glasgow, G2 4LD*. Tel. *041-332 7321*.

National Joint Council for the Building Industry
> EMPLOYERS' SEC. *Building Employers' Confederation, 82 New Cavandish Street, London, W1M 8AD*. Tel. *071-580 5588*
> OPERATIVES' SEC. *Union of Construction Allied Trades and Technicians, U.C.A.T.T. House, 177 Abbeville Road, Clapham, London, SW4 9RL*. Tel. *071-622 2442*
> CLERK TO THE COUNCIL. *18 Mansfield Street, London W1M 9FG*. Tel. *071-580 1740*

National Joint Council for the Engineering Construction Industry
> *The Secretary, Walmar House (6th Floor), 296 Regent Street, London, W1R 5HB*. Tel. *071 636 6291*

National Joint Council for Environmental Engineers and Allied Staffs
> EMPLOYERS' SEC. *F.S.C.A. House, 32–34 Palace Court, Bayswater, London, W2 4HY*. Tel. *071-229 1266*
> EMPLOYEES' SEC. *Hayes Court, West Common Road, Hayes, Bromley, Kent, BR2 7AU*. Tel. *081-462 7755*

National Joint Council for the Felt Roofing Contracting Industry
> EMPLOYERS' SEC. *Maxwelton House, Boltro Road, Haywards Heath, West Sussex, RH16 1BJ*. Tel. *440027 (STD code 0444)*
> WORKPEOPLES' SEC. *17 South Tay Street, Dundee*. Tel. *0382 26268*

National Joint Council for the Laying Side of the Mastic Asphalt Industry
> EMPLOYERS' SEC. *24 Weymouth Street, London, W1N 3FA*. Tel. *071 436 0102*.
> WORKPEOPLES' SEC. *A.U.A.W., Jenkin House, 173a Queen's Road, Peckham, London, SE15 2NF*. Tel. *071-639 1669*.

National Joint Council for the Thermal Insulation Contracting Industry
> EMPLOYERS' SEC. *Thermal Insulation Contractors Association, Kensway House, 388 High Road, Ilford, Essex, IG1 1TL*. Tel. *081-514 2120*
> WORKPEOPLE'S SEC. *GMB, 22–24 Worple Road, London SW19 4DD*. Tel. *081 947 3131*

National Joint Industrial Council for the Heating and Ventilating Contractors Association
> EMPLOYERS SEC. *E.S.C.A. House, 34 Palace Court, London, W2 4JG*. Tel. *071 229 2488 Ext. 213*
> EMPLOYEES SIDE. *M. S. F. 79 Camden Road, London, NW1 9ES*. Tel. *071-267 4422*

Scottish Joint Industry Board for the Electrical Contracting Industry
> JOINT SEC. *Electrical Contractors Association of Scotland, 23 Heriot Row, Edinburgh, EH3 6EW*. Tel. *031-225 7221*

Scottish and Northern Ireland Joint Industry Board for the Plumbing Industry
> JOINT SEC. *2 Walker Street, Edinburgh, EH3 7LB*. Tel. *031-225 2255*

Scottish Decorators Federation (Scottish Painting Council)
> EMPLOYERS' SEC. *249 West George Street, Glasgow, G2 4RB*. Tel. *041-221 7090*

Construction (continued)

WORKPEOPLE'S SEC. *U.C.A.T.T., 6 Fitzroy Place, Glasgow, G3 7RL.* Tel. *041-221 4893*

Works Services Trades Joint Council for Department of the Environment and Transport
OFFICIAL SIDE SEC. *Room A608, Whitgift Centre, Wellesley Road, Croydon, Surrey, CR9 3LY.* Tel. *081-760 4411*
TRADE UNION SIDE SEC. *Union of Construction, Allied Traders and Technicians, U.C.A.T.T. House, 177 Abbeville Road, Clapham, London, SW4 9RL.* Tel. *071-622 2442*

DISTRIBUTION, HOTELS, CATERING AND REPAIRS.

Wholesale Distribution

Food and Drink

Covent Garden Tenants Association Ltd.
EMPLOYERS' SEC. *F.C.A., Covent Garden Tenants' Association Ltd., A101 Fruit & Vegetable Market, New Covent Garden Market, London, SW8 5HH.* Tel. *071-720 7874*
WORKPEOPLE'S SEC. *Transport and General Workers Union, B170–171, Fruit and Vegetable Market, New Covent Garden Market, London, SW8 5HH.* Tel. *071-720 8344*

Joint Council for the Transport and Van Salesmen's Sections of the Baking Trade of Glasgow and West of Scotland
EMPLOYERS' SEC. *British Bakeries Ltd., 783 Duke Street, Glasgow, G31 1LL.* Tel. *041 556 5211.*
EMPLOYEES' SEC. *Trade Group Secretary, TGWU, 290 Bath Street, Glasgow, G2 4LD.* Tel. *041 332 7321*

Joint Industrial Council Representative of Employers and Workpeople connected with Slaughterhouses in the Meat Trade
EMPLOYERS' SEC. *Federation of Fresh Meat Wholesalers, 227 Central Markets, London, EC1A 9LH.* Tel. *071-329 0653*
WORKPEOPLE'S SEC. *Union of Shop, Distributive and Allied Workers, 188 Wilmslow Road, Manchester, M14 6LJ.* Tel. *061-224 2804*

Joint Industrial Council for the Wholesale Grocery and Provision Trade (England and Wales)
EMPLOYERS' SIDE. *Danish Bacon Company PLC, Denmark House, Parkway, Welwyn Garden City, Herts, AL8 6NN.* Tel. *07073 23421*
CHAIRMAN. *Malt House, Field End Road, Eastcote, Ruislip, Middx., HA4 9LW.* Tel. *081 422 9511*
WORKPEOPLE'S SEC. *Transport and General Workers' Union, Transport House, Smith Square, London, SW1P 3JB.* Tel. *071-828 7788*

Smithfield Market Tenants Association
EMPLOYERS' SEC. *Smithfield Market Tenants' Association, 225 Central Markets, London, EC1A 9LH.* Tel. *071-248 3151*
EMPLOYEES' SEC. *T.G.W.U. C153–155 Fruit and Vegetable Market, New Covent Garden Market, Vauxhall SW8 5HH.* Tel. *071-702 8344.*

Spitalfields Market Tenants Association Ltd.
EMPLOYERS' SEC. *Room 5, London Fruit Exchange, Brushfield Street, London, E1 6EP.* Tel. *071-247 5238*
WORKPEOPLE'S SEC. *1/511 Branch TGWU, 11 Lamb Street, London E1.* Tel. *071-247-2800*

Stratford Market Tenants Association Ltd
EMPLOYERS' SEC. *2 Stratford Market, London E15.* Tel. *081 519 5453.*

Western International Market Tenants' Association Limited
EMPLOYERS' SEC. *8, Market Centre, Western International Market, Hayes Road, Southall, Middlesex, UB2 5XR.* Tel. *081-573 5624*
WORKPEOPLE'S SEC. *Office No. 8, 14–15 Western International Market, Hayes Road, Southall, Middlesex, UB2 5XR.* Tel. *081-573 5624*

Wholesale Meat Agreement
EMPLOYERS SEC. *217 Central Markets, London, EC1A 9LH.* Tel. *071 489 0005*
EMPLOYEES SEC. *U.S.D.A.W., Oakley, 188 Wilmslow Road, Manchester, M14 6LJ.* Tel. *061 224 2804*

Scrap and Waste Materials

Joint Conciliation Committee for the Iron, Steel and Non-Ferrous Scrap Industry including Demolition, Dismantlement and Shipbreaking
EMPLOYERS' SEC. *16 High Street, Brampton, Huntingdon, PE18 8TU.* Tel. *Huntingdon 55249* (STD code 0480)

Wholesale Distribution (continued)

WORKPEOPLE'S SEC. *GMB, 22–24 Worple Road, London SW19 4DD*. Tel. *081 947 3131*

Miscellaneous Wholesalers

Joint Industrial Council Representative of Employers and Workpeople connected with the Hide and Skin Market Trade in England and Wales

EMPLOYERS' SEC. *National Federation of Hides and Skin Markets Inc. 51, Hill Avenue, Amersham, Bucks HP6 5BX*. Tel. *0494 728428.*

WORKPEOPLE'S SEC. *Textile Section, T.G.W.U., Transport House, Smith Square, London, SW1P 3JB*. Tel. *071-828 7788*

Retail Distribution

Food and Drink

Joint Industrial Council for the Retail Meat Trade

EMPLOYERS' SEC. *I Belgrove, Tunbridge Wells, Kent TN1 1YW*. Tel. *0892 414125*

WORKPEOPLE'S SEC. *U.S.D.A.W., "Oakley", 188 Wilmslow Road, Fallowfield, Manchester, M14 6LJ*. Tel. *061-224 2804*

Scottish Federation of Meat Traders' Associations (Inc.)

EMPLOYERS' SEC. *Scottish Federation of Meat Traders' Assoc.* (Inc). Hay's Auction Market, Needless Road, Perth PH2 0JW. Tel. *0738 37472.*

WORKPEOPLE'S SEC. *Union of Shop, Distributive and Allied Workers, "Muirfield", 342 Albert Drive, Glasgow, G41 5PG*. Tel. *041-427 6561*

Miscellaneous Retailers

National Concilliation Board for the Cooperative Service

EMPLOYERS' SEC. *Chief Industrial Relations Adviser, Co-operatives Employers Association, Holyoake House, Hanover Street, Manchester, M60 0AS*. Tel. *061-832 4300*

WORKPEOPLE'S SEC. *U.S.D.A.W., 188 wilmslow road, Fallowfield, Manchester, M14 6LJ.* Tel. *061-224 2804*

National Joint Council for the Motor Vehicle Retail and Repair Industry

EMPLOYERS' SEC *Motor Agents Association, 201 Great Portland Street, London, W1N 6AB.* Tel. *071-580 9122*

WORKPEOPLE'S SEC. *Transport and General Workers' Union, Vehicle Building and Auto Motive Group, Transport House, Smith Square, London, SW1P 3JB*. Tel. *071-828 7788*

National Joint Industrial Council for Retail Pharmacy (England and Wales)

EMPLOYERS' SEC. *National Pharmaceutical Association, 40–42 St. Peter's Street, St. Albans AL1 3NP*. Tel. *0727 32161 Ext. 247*

WORKPEOPLE'S SEC. *Union of Shop. Distributive and Allied Workers, "Oakley", 188 Wilmslow Road, Fallowfield, Manchester, M14 6LJ*. Tel. *061-224 2804*

TRANSPORT AND COMMUNICATION

Railways

British Transport Police Force Conference

The Secretary, British Railways Board Employee Relations Department, Euston House, 24 Eversholt Street, P.O. Box 100, London, NW1 1DZ. Tel. *071-922 6385*

The Secretary, B.T. Police Federation, Divisional HQ, Administration Offices, Paddington, London W2 1HF. Tel. *071 928 5151 Ext. 30117*

London Transport Executive Negotiating Committee (for Electrical Generation and Distribution Supervisory and Wages Staff)

The Secretary, London Underground Ltd., Signal and Electrical Engineering, 10A Wood Lane, London W12 7DT. Tel. *081-743-1152 Ext. 33*

WORKPEOPLE'S SEC. *Electrical, Electronic, Telecommunication and Plumbing Union, Hayes Court, West Common Road, Bromley, Kent BR2 7AU.*

Railway Negotiating Committee for Salaried and Concillation Staff

The Secretary, Dept. of the Personnel Director, London Underground Ltd., 55 Broadway, London, SW1H 0BD. Tel. *071-227 3216*

The Secretary, T.S.S.A., Walkden House, 10 Melton Street, London, NW1 2EJ. Tel. *071 387 2101.*

Railways *(continued)*

> *The Secretary, Unity House, Euston Road, London, NW1 2BL.* Tel. *071 387 4771.*
> *The Secretary, 9 Arkwright Road, Hampstead, London, NW3 6AB.* Tel. *071 431 0275.*

Railway Professional and Technical Staff National Council
> *The Secretary, British Railways Board Employee Relations Dept., Euston House, 24*
> *Eversholt Street, London NW1 1DZ.* Tel. *071-922 6385*
> *The Secretary, T.S.S.A., Walkden House, 10 Melton Street, London, NW1 2BL*

Railway Shopmen's National Council
> *The Secretary, British Railways Board Employee Relations Department, Euston House, 24*
> *Eversholt Street, London, NW1 1DZ.* Tel. *071-922 6385*
> *The Secretary, R.S.H.N.C., Unity House, Euston Road, London NW1 2BL.* Tel. *071 387*
> *4771*
> *A. Ferry, R.S.H.N.C., 140–142 Walworth Road, London SE17 1JW.* Tel. *071 703 2215*

Railway Staff National Council
> *The Secretary, British Railways Board Employee Relations Department, Euston House, 24*
> *Eversholt Street, P.O. Box 100, London, NW1 1DZ.* Tel. *071-922 6380*
> *The Secretary, T.S.S.A., Walkden House, 10 Melton Street, London NW1 2BL.* Tel. *071 387*
> *2101.*
> *The Secretary, Unity House, Euston Road, London NW1 2BL.* Tel. *071 387 4771.*
> *The Secretary, 9 Arkwright Road, Hampstead, London NW1 6AB.* Tel. *071 431 0275*

Railway Staff National Tribunal
> *The Secretary, A.C.A.S., 27 Wilton Street, London SW1X 7AZ.* Tel. *071-210 3625*

Railway Workshop Supervisory Staff National Council
> *The Secretary, British Railways Board Employee Relations Dept., Euston House, 24*
> *Eversholt Street, London, NW1 1DZ.* Tel. *071-922 6385*
> *The Secretary, R.W.S.S.J.N.C., Unity House, Euston Road, London NW1 2BL.* Tel. *071 387*
> *4771*

Special Joint Committee for the Machinery of Negotiation for Railway Staff
> *The Secretary, Room 533, British Railways Board Employee Relations Dept., Euston*
> *House, 24 Eversholt Street, London NW1 1DZ.* Tel. *071-922 6380*
> *The Secretary, Walkden House, 10 Melton Street, London NW1 2BL.* Tel. *071 387 2101*
> *The Secretary, N.U.R., Unity House, Euston Road, London NW1 2BL.* Tel. *071 387 4771*
> *The Secretary, 9 Arkwright Road, Hampstead, London NW3 6AB.* Tel. *071 431 0275*

Other Inland Transport

Joint Council for the Road Freight Industry (Northern Ireland)
> *The Secretary, 7 Belvoir Drive, Belfast, BT8 4BA.* Tel. *0232 642829.*
> *The Secretary, Amalgamated Transport and General Workers Union, Transport House, 102*
> *High Street, Belfast, BT1 2DL.* Tel. *232381* (STD code 0232)

Joint Negotiating Committee of the National Association of Inland Waterway Carriers
> *The Secretary, Fleet Chambers, 9/11 Jameson Street, Hull, HU1 3HR.* Tel. *0482 27281*
> *The Secretary, Transport and General Workers Union, Transport House, Smith Square,*
> *London SW1P 3JB.* Tel. *071 828 7788*

Joint Negotiating Committee for the Non-Manual Employees of Passenger Transport Executives
> *The Secretary, c/o West Yorkshire P.T.E., Metro House, West Parade, Wakefield, West*
> *Yorkshire, WF1 4TJ.* Tel. *0924 378234 Ext. 270*
> *The Secretary, Nalgo House, 1 Mabledon Place, London, WC1H 9AJ.* Tel. *071-388 2366*
> *Ext. 350*

National Joint Council for the British Waterways Salaried Staff
> *The Secretary, British Waterways Board, Willow Grange, Church Road, Watford,*
> *WD1 3QA.* Tel. *226422* (STD code 0923)
> *The Secretary, Nalgo House, 1 Mabledon Place, London, WC1H 9AJ.* Tel. *071-388 2366*

National Joint Council for British Waterways Wages Grades
> *The Secretary, 1 Dock Street, Leeds, LS1 1HH.* Tel. *0532 436741.*
> *The Secretary, Docks, Waterways and Fishing Group, T.G.W.U. Transport House, Smith*
> *Square, London, SW1P 3JB.* Tel. *071-828 7788*

National Joint Council for the Port Transport Industry
> *The Secretary, National Association of Port Employers, Commonwealth House, 1–19 New*
> *Oxford Street, London, WC1A 1DZ.* Tel. *071-242 1200*

Other Inland Transport *(continued)*

The Secretary, Transport and General Workers' Union, Transport House, Smith Square, London, SW1P 3JB. Tel. 071-828 7788
CLERK TO THE COUNCIL (to whom all correspondence should be addressed) *Miss S. E. Rudd, Commonwealth House, 1–19 New Oxford Street, London, WC1A 1DZ.*

Scottish Joint Industrial Council
The Secretary, Road Haulage Association Ltd., Roadway House, 17 Royal Terrace, Glasgow, G3 7NY. Tel. 041-332 9201
The Secretary, T.G.W.U., 290 Bath Street, Glasgow, G2 4LD. Tel. 041-332 7321

South Western Joint Industrial Council for Passenger Service Vehicle Operators in the Western Traffic Area
The Secretary, Coach Operators Federation, 23 High Street, Marshfield, Chippenham, Wilts, SN14 8LR. Tel. 0225 891324
The Secretary, Transport and General Workers' Union, Transport House, Victoria Street, Bristol, BS1 6AY. Tel. 230555 (STD code 0272)

Sea Transport

National Maritime Board
The Secretary, 30–32 St. Mary Axe, London, EC3A 8ET. Tel. 071-283 2922 Ext. 216
The Secretary, N.U.M.A.S.T., Ocean Air House, 750–760 High Road, Leytonstone, London E11 3BB. Tel. 081-989-6677.
The Secretary, National Union of Seamen, Maritime House, Old Town Clapham, London, SW4 0JP. Tel. 071-622 5581/6/8

Air Transport

National Joint Council for Civil Air Transport
The Secretary, Civil Air Transport Employers Secretariat, 121 Clare Road, Stanwell, Staines, Middlesex, TW19 7QP. Tel. (0784) 254034
The Secretary, B.A.L.P.A., 81 New Road, Harlington, Hayes, Middlesex, UB3 5BG. Tel. 081-759 9331

Supporting Services

Garston Docks Local Joint Committee
The Secretary, Associated British Ports, Dock Road, Garston, Liverpool, L19 2JW. Tel. 051-427 5971 Ext. 240
The Secretary, Transport and General Workers' Union, 4 Speke Road, Garston, Liverpool, L19 2PB. Tel. 051-427 7214

National Joint Committee (Automobile Association and A.A. Section APEX)
The Secretary, Automobile Association, Fanum House, Basing View, Basingstoke, Hampshire, RG21 2EA. Tel. 492973 (STD code 0256)
The Secretary, A.A. Section APEX, Thorne House, Queen Mary Avenue, Basingstoke, Hampshire. Tel. 464615 (STD code 0256)

South Wales Joint Control Board
The Secretary, Associated British Ports, Pierhead Building, Bute Docks, Cardiff, CF1 5TH. Tel. 0222 471311
The Secretary, T.G.W.U., Transport House, 1 Cathedral Road, Cardiff. Tel. 0222 394521.

Trinity House Joint Industrial Council
The Secretary, Lloyds Chambers (part 4th Floor), 1 Portsoken Street, London, E1 8BT. Tel. 071-480 6601
The Secretary, National Secretary Docks, Waterways and Fishing Group, T.G.W.U., Transport House, Smith Square, London, SW1P 3JB. Tel. 071-828 7788
The Secretary, NUMAST, 750-760 High Road, Leytonstone, London, E11 3BB.
The Secretary, G.M.B.T.U., 604 Green Lane, Goodmayes, Essex.

Postal and Telecommunications

National Joint Council of the Post Office Group and the Post Office Unions' Council
The Secretary, Room 220, Postal Headquarters, 33 Grosvenor Place, London, SW1X 1PX. Tel. 071-245 7200

Postal and Telecommunications *(continued)*

The Secretary, Post Office Union Council, Room 213, Alder House, 1 Aldersgate Street, London, EC1A 1AL. Tel. *071-606 6486*

Post Office Arbitration and Mediation Tribunal
The Secretary, ACAS, 27 Wilton Street, London SW1X 7AZ. Tel. *071-210 3625*

PUBLIC ADMINISTRATION

National Government

Civil Service National Whitley Council
OFFICIAL SIDE SEC. *H.M. Treasury, Treasury Chambers, Parliament Street, London, SW1P 3AG.* Tel. *071-270 4688*
TRADE UNION SIDE SEC. *Council of Civil Service Unions, 58 Rochester Row, London, SW1P 1JU.* Tel. *071-834 8393*

Departments of the Environment and Transport Departmental Joint Industrial Council
OFFICIAL SIDE SEC. *Dept. of the Environment, Property Service Agency, Room A604, Whitgift Centre, Wellesley Road, Croydon, Surrey, CR9 3LY.* Tel. *081 760 4415*
TRADE UNION SIDE SEC. *Union of Construction and Allied Technical Trades, 177 Abbeville Road, Clapham, London, SW4 9RL.* Tel. *071 622 2442*

Department of Trade and Industry Joint Industrial Council
OFFICIAL SIDE SEC. *Department of Trade and Industry, Room 808A, Bressendon Place, London, SW1E 5DT.* Tel. *071-215 3849*
TRADE UNION SIDE SEC. *Union of Construction and Allied Technical Trades, 177 Abbeville Road, Clapham, London, SW4 9RL.* Tel. *071-622 2442*

Engineering and Miscellaneous Trades Joint Council for Government Industrial Establishments
OFFICIAL SIDE SEC. *Room 315, Ministry of Defence, Sentinel House, 50–54 Southampton Row, London, WC1B 4AX.* Tel. *071-430 7536*
TRADE UNION SIDE SEC. *T.G.W.U., Transport House, Smith Square, London, SW1P 3JB.* Tel. *071-828 7788*

Joint Co-ordinating Committee for Government Industrial Establishments
OFFICIAL SIDE SEC. *H.M. Treasury, Pay 2 Division, Room 45A/3, Treasury Chambers, Parliament Street, London, SW1P 3AG.* Tel. *071-270 5591*
TRADE UNION SIDE SEC. *T.G.W.U., Transport House, Smith Square, London, SW1P 3JB.* Tel. *071-828-7788*

Ministry of Defence Joint Industrial Whitley Council
OFFICIAL SIDE SEC. *1/4 Room, 111, Northumberland House, Northumberland Ave, London, WC2N 5BP.* Tel. *071-218 0964.*
TRADE UNION SIDE SEC. *Ucatt House, 177 Abbeville Road, Clapham, London, SW4 9RL.* Tel. *071-622 2442*

Local Government

Joint Negotiating Committee for Chief Executives of Local Authorities
EMPLOYERS' SIDE SEC. *41 Belgrave Square, London, SW1X 8NZ.* Tel. *071-235 6081*
OFFICERS' SIDE SEC. *J.N.C. Chief Executives, East Sussex County Council, Pelham House, St. Andrews Lane, Lewes, BN7 1UN.* Tel. *0273 475400*

Joint Negotiating Committee for the Chief Officers of Local Authorities
AUTHORITIES SIDE SEC. *41 Belgrave Square, London, SW1X 8NZ.* Tel. *071-235 6081*
OFFICERS' SIDE SEC. *F.U.M.P.O. Offices, Terminus House, The High, Harlow, Essex, CM20 1TX.* Tel. *0279 34444*

Joint Negotiating Committee for Chief Officials of Local Authorities (Scotland)
EMPLOYERS' SEC. *F.I.P.M., F.B.I.M., F.I.T.D., Rosebery House, 9 Haymarket Terrace, Edinburgh, EH12 5XZ.* Tel. *031-346 1222*
WORKPEOPLE'S SEC. *c/o National Association of Local Government Officers, Hellenic House, 87–97 Bath Street, Glasgow, G2 2ER.* Tel. *041-332 0006*

Joint Negotiating Committee for Justices' Clerks
EMPLOYERS' SEC. *41 Belgrave Square, London, SW1X 8NZ.* Tel. *071-235 6081*

Local Government *(continued)*

OFFICERS' SIDE SEC. *Justices' Clerks' Society, 7C High Street, Barnet, EN5 5UE.* Tel. *081 441 9042*

Joint Negotiating Committee for Local Authorities' Services (Building and Civil Engineering)
EMPLOYERS' SEC. *41 Belgrave Square, London, SW1X 8NZ.* Tel. *071-235 6081*
OPERATIVES' SEC. *U.C.A.T.T. House, 177 Abbeville Road, London, SW4 9RL.* Tel. *071-622 2442*

Joint Negotiating Committee for Local Authorities' Services (Engineering Craftsmen)
EMPLOYERS' SEC. *41 Belgrave Square, London, SW1X 8NZ.* Tel. *071-235 6081*
WORKPEOPLE'S SEC. *Confederation of Shipbuilding and Engineering Unions, 140–142 Walworth Road, London, SE17 1JW.* Tel. *071-703 2215*

Joint Negotiating Committee for Magistrates Courts Staff
MANAGEMENT SIDE SEC. *41 Belgrave Square, London, SW1X 8NZ.* Tel. *071-235 6081*
OFFICERS' SIDE SEC. *Association of Magisterial Officers, 35 High Street, Crawley, West Sussex, RH10 1BQ.* Tel. *0293 547515/547516*

National Joint Council for Local Authorities Administrative Professional Technical & Clerical Services, (Residential and Allied Staffs Committee)
EMPLOYERS' SEC. *41 Belgrave Square, London, SW1X 8NZ.* Tel. *071-235 6081*
STAFF SIDE SEC. *N.A.L.G.O., 1 Mabledon Place, London, WC1H 9AJ.* Tel. *071-388 2366*

National Joint Council for Chief and Assistant Chief Officers of Local Authorities' Fire Brigades
EMPLOYERS' SEC. *41 Belgrave Square, London, SW1X 8NZ.* Tel. *071-235 6081*
STAFF SIDE SEC. *C.A.C.F.O.A., Hampshire Fire Service H.Q., Leigh Road, Eastleigh, Hants, SO5 4JS.* Tel. *0703 620000*

National Joint Council for Local Authorities' Administrative, Professional, Technical and Clerical Services
EMPLOYERS' SEC. *41 Belgrave Square, London, SW1X 8NZ.* Tel. *071-235 6081*
STAFF SIDE SEC. *Nalgo House, 1 Mabledon Place, London, WC1H 9AJ.* Tel. *071-388 2366*

National Joint Council for Local Authorities' A.P.T. and C. Services (Scottish Council)
EMPLOYERS' SEC. *F.I.P.M., F.B.I.M., F.I.T.D., Rosebery House, 9 Haymarket Terrace, Edinburgh, EH12 5XZ.* Tel. *031-346 1222*
WORKPEOPLE'S SEC. *c/o National Association of Local Government Officers, Hellenic House, 87–97 Bath Street, Glasgow, G2 2ER.* Tel. *041-332 0006*

National Joint Council for Local Authorities' Fire Brigades
EMPLOYERS' SEC. *41 Belgrave Square, London, SW1X 8NZ.* Tel. *071-235 6081*
EMPLOYEE'S SEC. *Fire Brigades Union, Bradley House, 68 Coombe Road, Kingston-Upon-Thames, Surrey, KT2 7AE.* Tel. *081-541 1765*

National Joint Council for Local Authorities' Services (Manual Workers)
EMPLOYERS' SEC. *41 Belgrave Square, London, SW1X 8NZ.* Tel. *071-235 6081*
WORKPEOPLE'S SEC *G.M.B.A.T.U., Thorne House, Ruxley Ridge, Claygate, Esher, Surrey, KT10 0TL.* Tel. *0372 62081*

National Joint Council for Local Authorities' Service (Manual Workers) (Scottish Council)
EMPLOYERS' SEC. *F.I.P.M., F.B.I.M., F.I.T.D., Rosebery House, 9 Haymarket Terrace, Edinburgh, EH12 5XZ.* Tel. *031-346 1222*
WORKPEOPLE'S SEC. *Fountain House, 1/3 Woodside Crescent, Glasgow, G3 7UJ.* Tel. *041-332-8641.*

Northern Ireland Joint Council for Local Authorities' Administrative, Professional, Technical and Clerical Services
EMPLOYERS' SEC. *City Hall, Belfast, BT1 5GS.* Tel. *(0232) 320202*
WORKPEOPLE'S SEC. *Northern Ireland Public Service Alliance, Harkin House, 54 Wellington Park, Belfast, BT9 6BZ.* Tel. *661831* (STD code 0232)

Northern Ireland Joint Industrial Council for Local Authorities Services (Manual Workers)
EMPLOYERS' SEC *City Hall, Belfast, BT1 5GS.* Tel. *(0232) 320202*
EMPLOYEES' SEC. *A.T.G.W.U., 1A Dromore Street, Banbridge, BT32 4BS.* Tel. *(082 06) 23680.*

Scottish Joint Negotiating Committee for Local Authorities' Services (Building and Civil Engineering)
EMPLOYERS' SEC. *F.I.P.M., F.B.I.M., F.I.T.D., Rosebery House, 9 Haymarket Terrace, Edinburgh, EH12 5XZ.* Tel. *031-346 1222*

Local Government *(continued)*

WORKPEOPLE'S SEC. *6 Fitzroy Place, Glasgow, G3 7RL. Tel. 041-221 4893.*

Scottish Joint Negotiating Committee for Local Authorities Services (Engineering Craftsmen)
EMPLOYERS SEC. *F.I.P.M., F.B.I.M., F.I.T.D., Rosebery House, 9 Haymarket Terrace, Edinburgh, EH12 5XZ. Tel. 031 346 1222*
WORKPEOPLE'S SEC. *145 Morrison Street, Edinburgh, EH3 8AL. Tel. 031-229 8711*

Scottish Joint Negotiating Committee for Local Authorities' Services (Craftsmen)
EMPLOYERS' SEC. *F.I.P.M., F.B.I.M., F.I.T.D., Rosebery House, 9 Haymarket Terrace, Edinburgh, EH12 5XZ. Tel. 031-346 1222*
WORKPEOPLE'S SEC. *17 South Tay Street, Dundee, DD1 1NR. Tel. 0382 26268*

Scottish Joint Negotiating Committee for Local Authorities Water Supply Services (Manual Workers)
EMPLOYERS SEC. *F.I.P.M., F.B.I.M., F.I.T.D., Rosebery House, 9 Haymarket Terrace, Edinburgh, EH12 5XZ. Tel. 031-346 1222*
WORKPEOPLE'S SEC. *Fountain House, 1–3 Woodside Crescent, Glasgow, G3 7UJ. Tel. 041-332 8641.*

The Whitley Council for New Towns Staff
EMPLOYERS' SEC. *41 Belgrave Square, London SW1X 8NZ. Tel. 071-235 6081*
STAFF SIDE SEC. *N.A.L.G.O., 1 Mabledon Place, London, WC1H 9AJ. Tel. 071-388 2366*

Police

Police Arbitration Tribunal
The Secretary, A.C.A.S. 27 Wilton Street, London, SW1X 7AZ. Tel. 071-210 3625

EDUCATION

Joint Negotiating Committee for Teachers in Social Service Establishments
EMPLOYERS' SEC. *41 Belgrave Square, London, SW1X 8NZ. Tel. 071-235 6081*
STAFF SIDE SEC. *N.U.T., Hamilton House, Mabledon Place, London, WC1H 9BD. Tel. 071-388 6191*

Joint Committee for Clerical and Certain Related Administrative Staff
EMPLOYERS' SEC. *29 Tavistock Square, London, WC1H 9EZ. Tel. 071-387 9231*
EMPLOYERS' SEC. *N.A.L.G.O., 1 Mabledon Place, London, WC1H 9AJ. Tel. 071-388 2366*

Joint Committee for Manual and Ancillary Staffs
EMPLOYERS' SEC. *U.C.N.S., 29 Tavistock Square, London, WC1H 9EZ. Tel. 071-387 9231.*
EMPLOYEES' SEC. *N.U.P.E., Civic House, 20 Grand Depot Road, Woolwich, London, SE18 6SF. Tel. 081-854-2244*

Joint Committee for Technical Staffs (Universities)
EMPLOYERS' SEC. *U.C.N.S., Tavistock House South, 29 Tavistock Square, London, WC1H 9EZ. Tel. 071-387 9231*
EMPLOYEE'S SEC. *Manufacturing Science Finance, 79 Camden Road, London, NW1 9ES.*

National Employer's Organisation—School Teachers
MANAGEMENT PANEL SEC. *41 Belgrave Square, London, SW1X 8NZ. Tel. 071-235 6081*

National Joint Council for Lecturers in Further Education in England and Wales
MANAGEMENT PANEL SEC. *41 Belgrave Square, London, SW1X 8NZ. Tel. 071-235 6081*
TEACHERS' PANEL *N.A.T.F.H.E., 27 Britannia Street, London, WC1X 9JP. Tel. 071-837 3636*

Scottish Joint Negotiating Committee for Teaching Staff in Further Education
AUTHORITIES' SIDE SEC. *F.I.P.M., F.B.I.M., F.I.T.D., Rosebery House, 9 Haymarket Terrace, Edinburgh, EH12 5XZ. Tel. 031-346 1222*
TEACHERS' SEC. *46 Moray Place, Edinburgh, EH3 6BH. Tel. 031-225 6244.*

Scottish Joint Negotiating Committee for Teaching Staff in School Education
MANAGEMENT SIDE SEC. *F.I.P.M., F.B.I.M., F.I.T.D., Rosebery House, 9 Haymarket Terrace, Edinburgh, EH12 5XZ. Tel. 031-346 1222*
TEACHERS' SEC. *Educational Institute of Scotland, 46 Moray Place, Edinburgh, EH3 6BH. Tel. 031-225 6244*

Education *(continued)*

Soulbury Committee (Inspectors, Organisers and Advisory Officers of Local Education
    Authorities)
    MANAGEMENT PANEL SEC. *41 Belgrave Square, London, SW1X 8NZ.* Tel. *071-235 6081*
    OFFICERS' PANEL SEC. *N.U.T., Hamilton House, Mabledon Place, London, WC1H 9BD.* Tel.
    071-388 6191

MEDICAL AND HEALTH SERVICES

Administrative and Clerical Staffs Council, Ambulance Officers Joint Negotiating Committee
    MANAGEMENT SIDE SEC. *Room 1206, Hannibal House, Elephant and Castle, London,*
    SE1 6TE. Tel. *071-703 6380 Ext. 3653.*
    STAFF SIDE SEC. *Nalgo House, 1 Mabledon Place, London, WC1H 9AJ.* Tel. *071-388 2366*
    Ext. 357.

Ambulance Whitley Council
    MANAGEMENT SIDE SEC. *Room 1206, Hannibal House, Elephant and Castle, London,*
    SE1 6TE. Tel. *071-703 6380 Ext. 3653*
    STAFF SIDE SEC. *N.U.P.E., Civic House, 20 Grand Depot Road, Woolwich, London,*
    SE18 6SF. Tel. *081-854 2244.*

Ancillary Staffs Council of the Whitley Councils for the Health Services (Great Britain)
    MANAGEMENT SIDE SEC. *Room 36, Hannibal House, Elephant and Castle, London,*
    SE1 6TE. Tel. *071-703 6380 Ext. 139*
    STAFF SIDE SEC. *National Union of Public Employees, Civic House, 20 Grand Depot Road,*
    Woolwich, London, SE18 6SF. Tel. *081 854-2244.*

General Whitley Council for the Health Services (G.B.)
    MANAGEMENT SIDE SEC. *Room 1112, Hannibal House, Elephant and Castle, London,*
    SE1 6TE. Tel. *071-703 6380 Ext. 3614*
    STAFF SIDE SEC. *Nalgo House, 1 Mabledon Place, London, WC1H 9AJ.* Tel. *071-388 2366*
    Ext. 352

Joint Negotiating Body for Doctors in Community Medicine and the Community Health Services
    MANAGEMENT SIDE SEC. *Department of Health, Room 428, Portland Court, 158–176 Great*
    Portland Street, London, W1N 5TB. Tel. *071-872 9302 Ext. 48274*
    STAFF SIDE SEC. *British Medical Association, B.M.A. House, Tavistock Square, London,*
    WC1H 9JP. Tel. *071-387 4499*

Joint Negotiating Committee for Hospital Medical and Dental Staff (Seniors)
    JOINT MANAGEMENT SIDE SEC. *Department of Health, Room 428 Portland Court, 158–176*
    Great Portland Street, London, W1N 5TB. Tel. *071-872 9302 Ext. 48274*
    STAFF SIDE SEC. *B.M.A. House, British Medical Association, Tavistock Square, WC1H 9JP.*
    Tel. *071-387 4499*
    Junior Doctors Only
    EMPLOYERS SEC. *Room 429, Portland Court, 158–176 Great Portland Street, London,*
    W1N 5TB. Tel. *071-872 9302 Ext. 48275*
    EMPLOYEES SEC. *B.M.A. House, British Medical Association, Tavistock Square, WC1H 9JP.*
    Tel. *071-383 6237.*

Joint Negotiating Forum for Community Dental Services
    MANAGEMENT SIDE SEC. *Department of Health, Portland Court, 158–176 Portland Street,*
    London, W1N 5TB. Tel. *071-872 9302 Ext. 48356.*
    STAFF SIDE SEC. *British Dental Association, 64 Wimpole Street, London, W1M 8AL.* Tel.
    071-935 0875

Management Advisory Panel for N.H.S. Maintenance Staff
    EMPLOYERS SEC. *Room 1206, Hannibal House, Elephant and Castle, London, SE1 6TE.*
    Tel. *071-703 6380 Ext. 3653*
    WORKPEOPLE'S SEC. *E.E.T.P.U., Hayes Court, West Common Road, Bromley, Kent,*
    BR2 7AU. Tel. *081-462 7755.*

Nursing and Midwifery Staffs Negotiating Council
    MANAGEMENT SIDE SEC. *Department of Health, Room 1205, Hannibal House, Elephant*
    and Castle, London, SE1 6TE. Tel. *071-703 6380 Ext. 3426*
    STAFF SIDE SEC. *Royal College of Nursing, 20 Cavendish Square, London, W1M 0AB.* Tel.
    071-491 4447

Medical and Health Services *(continued)*

Optical Whitley Council (Committees A and B)
> MANAGEMENT SIDE SEC. *Department of Health, Hannibal House, Elephant and Castle, London, SE1 6TE. Tel. 071-703 6380 Ext. 3982*
> STAFF SIDE SEC. *Association of Optometrists, Bridge House, 233–234 Blackfriars Road, London, SE1 8NW. Tel. 071-261-9661*

Pharmaceutical Whitley Council Committe A
> MANAGEMENT SIDE SEC. *Department of Health, Hannibal House, Elephant and Castle, London, SE1 6TE. Tel. 071-703 6380 Ext. 3982*
> STAFF SIDE SEC. *6 Stanley Street, Liverpool, L1 6AF. Tel. 051-236 3511*

Professional and Technical Staffs "B" Whitley Council for Health Services (G.B.)
> MANAGEMENT SIDE SEC. *Room 1107, Hannibal House, Elephant and Castle, London, SE1 6TE. Tel. 071-703-6380 Ext 3342*
> STAFF SIDE SEC. *C.O.H.S.E., Glen House, High St., Banstead, Surrey, SM7 2LH. Tel. 07373-53322*

Professions Allied to Medicine (P.T.A.) Council
> EMPLOYERS SIDE. *Department of Health, Room 1208 Hannibal House, London SE1 6TE. Tel. 071-703 6380 ext. 3643*
> EMPLOYEES SIDE. *Chartered Society of Physiotherapy, 14 Bedford Row, London WC1R 4ED. Tel. 071-242 1941*

Scientific and Professional Staffs Whitley Council
> MANAGEMENT SIDE SEC *D.H.S.S., Room 81, Hannibal House, Elephant and Castle, SE1 6TE. Tel. 071-703 6380 Ext. 3982*
> JOINT STAFF SIDE SECS. *78 St. Pancras Way, London, NW1 9NZ. Tel. 071-485 4064. Dr. J. A. R. McIntosh, Dept. of Clinical Physics and Bioengineering, Walsgrave Hospital, Clifford Bridge Road, Walsgrave, Coventry CV2 2DX. Tel. 0203 602020 Ext. 84444. The Secretary, N.A.L.G.O., 1 Mabledon Place, London, WC1H 9AJ. Tel. 071-388 2366*

Whitley Councils for the Health Services (Great Britain) Administrative and Clerical Staffs Council
> MANAGEMENT SIDE SEC. *Room 1113, Hannibal House, Elephant and Castle, London, SE1 6TE. Tel. 071-703 6380 Ext 3979*
> STAFF SIDE SEC. *Nalgo House, 1 Mabledon Place, London, WC1H 9AJ. Tel. 071-388 2366*

Northern Ireland—Joint Councils for the Health and Personal Social Services

Administrative and Clerical Staffs' Joint Council
> *Management Side Secy., Dundonald House, Upper Newtownards Road, Belfast, BT4 3SF. Tel. Belfast 650111 Ext. 260.*
> *Staff Side Secy., N.I.P.S.A., 54 Wellington Park, Belfast, BT9 6DZ. Tel. Belfast 661831.*

Ambulance Staffs' Joint Council
> *Management Side Secy., Dundonald House, Upper Newtownards Road, Belfast, BT4 3SF. Tel. Belfast 650111.*
> *Staff Side Secy., N.U.P.E., 523 Antrim Road, Belfast BT15 3BS. Tel. 776971/770813/777684/777210.*

Ancillary and General Staffs' Joint Council
> *Management Side Secretary, Dundonald House, Upper Newtownards Road, Belfast, BT4 3SF. Tel. 650111.*
> *Staff Side Secy., C.O.H.S.E., 27 Ulsterville Avenue, Lisburn Road, Belfast BT9 7AS. Tel. Belfast 662994.*

Maintenance Staffs' Joint Council
> *Management Side Secy., Dundonald House, Upper Newtownards Road, Belfast BT4 3SF. Tel. Belfast 650111.*
> *Staff Side Secy., C.O.H.S.E., 27 Ulsterville Avenue, Lisburn Road, Belfast, BT9 7AS. Tel. 662994.*

Nurses and Midwives Staffs' Joint Council
> *Management Side Secy., Dundonald House, Upper Newtownards Road, Belfast, BT4 3SF. Tel. Belfast 650111.*
> *Staff Side Secy., C.O.H.S.E., 27 Ulsterville Avenue, Lisburn Road, Belfast, BT9 7AS. Tel. 662994.*

Northern Ireland—Joint Councils for the Health and Personal Social Services *(continued)*

Professional and Technical Staffs' Joint Council
> *Management Side Secy., Dundonald House, Upper Newtownards Road, Belfast, BT4 3SF.* Tel. *650111.*
> *Staff Side Secy., C.O.H.S.E., 27 Ulsterville Avenue, Lisburn Road, Belfast, BT9 7AS.* Tel. *662994.*

Social Work Staffs' Joint Council
> *Management Side Secy., Dundonald House, Upper Newtownards Road, Belfast, BT4 3SF.* Tel. *Belfast 650111.*
> *Staff Side Secy., N.I.P.S.A., 54 Wellington Park, Belfast, BT9 6DZ.* Tel. *Belfast 661831.*

General Council
> *Management Side Secy., Dundonald House, Upper Newtownards Road, Belfast, BT4 3SF.* Tel. *Belfast 650111.*
> *Staff Side Secy., C.O.H.S.E., 27 Ulsterville Avenue, Lisburn Road, Belfast, BT9 7AS.* Tel. *662994.*

MISCELLANEOUS SERVICES

Recreational and Cultural Services

Joint Council for the Regulation of Employment and Negotiation of Wages and Conditions for Crowd Artistes
> EMPLOYERS' SEC. *Paramount House, 162–170 Wardour St., London, W1V 4LA.* Tel. *071 494 4965*
> WORKPEOPLE'S SEC. *Film Artistes Association, 61 Marloes Road, Kensington, London, W8 6LF.* Tel. *071-937 4567*

National Joint Council for Stable Staff
> EMPLOYER'S SEC. *Cooksey Farm, Upton Warren, Bromsgrove, Worcs., B51 9ER.* Tel. *029-923 612*
> EMPLOYEE'S SEC. *Transport House, Smith Square, London, SW1P 3JB.* Tel. *071-828 7788*
> *The Secretary, Stable Lads Assoc., The Granary, Harcombe House, Chasleton, Moreton-in-the-Marsh, Glos.* Tel. *0608-74293*

Variety and Allied Entertainments Council of Great Britain
> EMPLOYERS' SEC. *04 Keyes House, Dolphin Square, London, SW1V 3NA.* Tel. *071-834-0515*
> WORKPEOPLE'S SEC. *British Actors Equity Association, 8 Harley Street, London, W1N 2AB.* Tel. *071-636 6367*

Other Services

Joint Negotiating Committee for Youth and Community Workers
> EMPLOYERS' PANEL SEC. *41 Belgrave Square, London, SW1X 8NZ.* Tel. *071-235 6081*
> STAFF PANEL SEC. *N.U.T., Hamilton House, Mabledon Place, London, WC1H 9BD.* Tel. *071-388 6191*

Joint Negotiating Committee for the Probation Service
> EMPLOYERS' SEC. *41 Belgrave Square, London, SW1X 8NZ.* Tel. *071-235 6081*
> WORKPEOPLE'S SEC. *National Association of Probation Officers, 3–4 Chivalry Road, London, SW11 1HT.* Tel. *071-223 4887*

NATIONAL ORGANISATIONS COVERING VARIOUS INDUSTRIES

National Joint Council for Workshops for the Blind
> EMPLOYERS' SEC. *41 Belgrave Square, London, SW1X 8NZ.* Tel. *071-235 6081*
> STAFF SIDE SEC. *National League of the Blind and Disabled, 2 Tenterden Road, London, N17 8BE.* Tel. *081-808 6030*

*

WAGES COUNCILS

GREAT BRITAIN

Secretary, Office of Wages Councils, 222 Grays Inn Road,
London, WC1X 8HL. Tel. 071-211 4048 Fax. 071 211 4456

Aerated Waters
Boot and Shoe Repairing
Button Manufacturing
Clothing Manufacturing
Coffin Furniture and Cerement Making
Cotton Waste Reclamation
Flax and Hemp
Fur
General Waste Materials Reclamation
Hairdressing Undertakings
Hat, Cap and Millinery
Lace Finishing
Laundry
Licensed Non-residential Establishment
Licensed Residential Establishment and Licensed Restaurant
Linen and Cotton Handkerchief and Household Goods and Linen Piece Goods
Made-up Textiles
Ostrich and Fancy Feather and Artificial Flower
Perambulator and Invalid Carriage
Retail Bespoke Tailoring
Retail Food and Allied Trades
Retail Trades Non-food
Rope, Twine and Net
Sack and Bag
Toy Manufacturing
Unlicensed Place of Refreshment

NORTHERN IRELAND

Office of Wages Councils, 83 Ladas Drive, Belfast, BT6 9FJ.
Tel. 0232 401520

Baking
Boot and Shoe Repairing
Catering
Clothing
Laundry
Linen and Cotton Handkerchief and Household Goods and Linen Piece Goods
Paper Box
Road Haulage
Sugar Confectionery and Food Preserving

AGRICULTURAL WAGES BOARDS

Agricultural Wages Board for England and Wales

The Secretary, Eagle House, 90–96 Cannon Street, London, EC4N 6HT. Tel. 071-623 4266

Scottish Agricultural Wages Board

The Secretary, Chesser House, 500 Gorgie Road, Edinburgh, EG11 3AW. Tel. 031-443 4020 Ext. 2469

Agricultural Wages Board for Northern Ireland

The Secretary, Department of Agriculture, Magnet House, 81–93 York Street, Belfast, BT15 1AD. Tel. 224681 (STD code 0232)

CENTRAL ARBITRATION COMMITTEE

The Secretary, 39 Grosvenor Place, London, SW1X 7BD. Tel. 071-210 3737/3738/3741

CIVIL SERVICE ARBITRATION TRIBUNAL

The Secretary, 22 Kingsway, London, WC2 B6JY. Tel. 071-405-5944

INDUSTRIAL COURT NORTHERN IRELAND

Industrial Court, 2nd Floor, Bedford House, 16–22 Bedford Street, Belfast, BT2 7NR. Tel. 0232 327666

CENTRAL OFFICE OF INDUSTRIAL TRIBUNALS

England and Wales

93 Ebury Bridge Road, London, SW1W 8RE. Tel. 071-730 9161

Northern Ireland

2nd Floor, Bedford House, Bedford Street, Belfast, BT2 7NR. Tel. 0232 327666

Scotland

St. Andrew House, 141 West Nile Street, Glasgow, G1 2RU. Tel. 041-331 1601

ADVISORY CONCILIATION AND ARBITRATION SERVICE

D. B. Smith C.B., 27 Wilton Street, London, SW1X 7AZ. Tel. 071-210 3625

LABOUR RELATIONS AGENCY

Windsor House, 9–15 Bedford Street, Belfast, BT2 7NU. Tel. 0232 321442

FRIENDLY SOCIETIES REGISTRY (NORTHERN IRELAND)

Department of Economic Development, IDB House, 64 Chichester Street, Belfast, BT1 4JK. Tel. 234488 (STD code 0232)

CERTIFICATION OFFICE FOR TRADE UNIONS AND EMPLOYERS' ASSOCIATIONS

27 Wilton Street, London, SW1X 7AZ. Tel. 071-210 3733/4

INDEX

Printed in the United Kingdom for HMSO
Dd297294 3/94 C8 G531 10170